Scott Foresman SCIENCE

Series Authors

Dr. Timothy Cooney
Professor of Earth Science and Science Education
Earth Science Department
University of Northern Iowa
Cedar Falls, Iowa

Michael Anthony DiSpezio
Science Education Specialist
Cape Cod Children's Museum
Falmouth, Massachusetts

Barbara K. Foots
Science Education Consultant
Houston, Texas

Dr. Angie L. Matamoros
Science Curriculum Specialist
Broward County Schools
Ft. Lauderdale, Florida

Kate Boehm Nyquist
Science Writer and Curriculum Specialist
Mount Pleasant, South Carolina

Dr. Karen L. Ostlund
Professor
Science Education Center
The University of Texas at Austin
Austin, Texas

Contributing Authors

Dr. Anna Uhl Chamot
Associate Professor and ESL Faculty Advisor
Department of Teacher Preparation and Special Education
Graduate School of Education and Human Development
The George Washington University
Washington, D.C.

Dr. Jim Cummins
Professor
Modern Language Centre and Curriculum Department
Ontario Institute for Studies in Education
Toronto, Canada

Gale Philips Kahn
Lecturer, Science and Math Education
Elementary Education Department
California State University, Fullerton
Fullerton, California

Vincent Sipkovich
Teacher
Irvine Unified School District
Irvine, California

Steve Weinberg
Science Consultant
Connecticut State Department of Education
Hartford, Connecticut

PEARSON Scott Foresman
Editorial Offices: Glenview, Illinois • Parsippany, New Jersey • New York, New York
Sales Offices: Boston, Massachusetts • Duluth, Georgia • Glenview, Illinois
Coppell, Texas • Sacramento, California • Mesa, Arizona

Content Consultants

Dr. J. Scott Cairns
National Institutes of Health
Bethesda, Maryland

Jackie Cleveland
Elementary Resource Specialist
Mesa Public School District
Mesa, Arizona

Robert L. Kolenda
Science Lead Teacher, K-12
Neshaminy School District
Langhorne, Pennsylvania

David P. Lopath
Teacher
The Consolidated School District
   of New Britain
New Britain, Connecticut

Sammantha Lane Magsino
Science Coordinator
Institute of Geophysics
University of Texas at Austin
Austin, Texas

Kathleen Middleton
Director, Health Education
ToucanEd
Soquel, California

Irwin Slesnick
Professor of Biology
Western Washington University
Bellingham, Washington

Dr. James C. Walters
Professor of Geology
University of Northern Iowa
Cedar Falls, Iowa

Multicultural Consultants

Dr. Shirley Gholston Key
Assistant Professor
University of Houston-Downtown
Houston, Texas

Damon L. Mitchell
Quality Auditor
Louisiana-Pacific Corporation
Conroe, Texas

Classroom Reviewers

Kathleen Avery
Teacher
Kellogg Science/Technology Magnet
Wichita, Kansas

Margaret S. Brown
Teacher
Cedar Grove Primary
Williamston, South Carolina

Deborah Browne
Teacher
Whitesville Elementary School
Moncks Corner, South Carolina

Wendy Capron
Teacher
Corlears School
New York, New York

Jiwon Choi
Teacher
Corlears School
New York, New York

John Cirrincione
Teacher
West Seneca Central Schools
West Seneca, New York

Jacqueline Colander
Teacher
Norfolk Public Schools
Norfolk, Virginia

Dr. Terry Contant
Teacher
Conroe Independent
   School District
The Woodlands, Texas

Susan Crowley-Walsh
Teacher
Meadowbrook Elementary School
Gladstone, Missouri

Charlene K. Dindo
Teacher
Fairhope K-1 Center/Pelican's Nest
   Science Lab
Fairhope, Alabama

Laurie Duffee
Teacher
Barnard Elementary
Tulsa, Oklahoma

Beth Anne Ebler
Teacher
Newark Public Schools
Newark, New Jersey

Karen P. Farrell
Teacher
Rondout Elementary School
   District #72
Lake Forest, Illinois

Anna M. Gaiter
Teacher
Los Angeles Unified School District
   Los Angeles Systemic Initiative
Los Angeles, California

Federica M. Gallegos
Teacher
Highland Park Elementary
Salt Lake School District
Salt Lake City, Utah

Janet E. Gray
Teacher
Anderson Elementary - Conroe ISD
Conroe, Texas

Karen Guinn
Teacher
Ehrhardt Elementary School - KISD
Spring, Texas

Denis John Hagerty
Teacher
Al Ittihad Private Schools
Dubai, United Arab Emirates

Judith Halpern
Teacher
Bannockburn School
Deerfield, Illinois

Debra D. Harper
Teacher
Community School District 9
Bronx, New York

Gretchen Harr
Teacher
Denver Public Schools - Doull School
Denver, Colorado

Bonnie L. Hawthorne
Teacher
Jim Darcy School
School District #1
Helena, Montana

Marselle Heywood-Julian
Teacher
Community School District 6
New York, New York

Scott Klene
Teacher
Bannockburn School 106
Bannockburn, Illinois

Thomas Kranz
Teacher
Livonia Primary School
Livonia, New York

Tom Leahy
Teacher
Coos Bay School District
Coos Bay, Oregon

Mary Littig
Teacher
Kellogg Science/Technology Magnet
Wichita, Kansas

Patricia Marin
Teacher
Corlears School
New York, New York

Susan Maki
Teacher
Cotton Creek CUSD 118
Island Lake, Illinois

Efraín Meléndez
Teacher
East LA Mathematics Science
   Center LAUSD
Los Angeles, California

Becky Mojalid
Teacher
Manarat Jeddah Girls' School
Jeddah, Saudi Arabia

Susan Nations
Teacher
Sulphur Springs Elementary
Tampa, Florida

Brooke Palmer
Teacher
Whitesville Elementary
Moncks Corner, South Carolina

Jayne Pedersen
Teacher
Laura B. Sprague
   School District 103
Lincolnshire, Illinois

Shirley Pfingston
Teacher
Orland School District 135
Orland Park, Illinois

Teresa Gayle Rountree
Teacher
Box Elder School District
Brigham City, Utah

Helen C. Smith
Teacher
Schultz Elementary
Klein Independent School District
Tomball, Texas

Denette Smith-Gibson
Teacher
Mitchell Intermediate, CISD
The Woodlands, Texas

Mary Jean Syrek
Teacher
Dr. Charles R. Drew Science
   Magnet
Buffalo, New York

Rosemary Troxel
Teacher
Libertyville School District 70
Libertyville, Illinois

Susan D. Vani
Teacher
Laura B. Sprague School
School District 103
Lincolnshire, Illinois

Debra Worman
Teacher
Bryant Elementary
Tulsa, Oklahoma

Dr. Gayla Wright
Teacher
Edmond Public School
Edmond, Oklahoma

ISBN: 0-328-26835-6
2008 Edition
Copyright © 2003, Pearson Education, Inc.
All Rights Reserved. Printed in the United States of America. This publication is protected by Copyright, and permission should be obtained from the publisher prior to any prohibited reproduction, storage in a retrieval system, or transmission in any form by any means, electronic, mechanical, photocopying, recording, or otherwise. For information regarding permission(s), write to: Permissions Department, Scott Foresman, 1900 East Lake Avenue, Glenview, Illinois 60025.

1 2 3 4 5 6 7 8 9 10 V063 13 12 11 10 09 08 07 06

Activity and Safety Consultants

Laura Adams
Teacher
Holley-Navarre Intermediate
Navarre, Florida

Dr. Charlie Ashman
Teacher
Carl Sandburg Middle School
Mundelein District #75
Mundelein, Illinois

Christopher Atlee
Teacher
Horace Mann Elementary
Wichita Public Schools
Wichita, Kansas

David Bachman
Consultant
Chicago, Illinois

Sherry Baldwin
Teacher
Shady Brook
Bedford ISD
Euless, Texas

Pam Bazis
Teacher
Richardson ISD
 Classical Magnet School
Richardson, Texas

Angela Boese
Teacher
McCollom Elementary
Wichita Public Schools USD #259
Wichita, Kansas

Jan Buckelew
Teacher
Taylor Ranch Elementary
Venice, Florida

Shonie Castaneda
Teacher
Carman Elementary, PSJA
Pharr, Texas

Donna Coffey
Teacher
Melrose Elementary - Pinellas
St. Petersburg, Florida

Diamantina Contreras
Teacher
J.T. Brackenridge Elementary
San Antonio ISD
San Antonio, Texas

Susanna Curtis
Teacher
Lake Bluff Middle School
Lake Bluff, Illinois

Karen Farrell
Teacher
Rondout Elementary School,
 Dist. #72
Lake Forest, Illinois

Paul Gannon
Teacher
El Paso ISD
El Paso, Texas

Nancy Garman
Teacher
Jefferson Elementary School
Charleston, Illinois

Susan Graves
Teacher
Beech Elementary
Wichita Public Schools USD #259
Wichita, Kansas

Jo Anna Harrison
Teacher
Cornelius Elementary
Houston ISD
Houston, Texas

Monica Hartman
Teacher
Richard Elementary
Detroit Public Schools
Detroit, Michigan

Kelly Howard
Teacher
Sarasota, Florida

Kelly Kimborough
Teacher
Richardson ISD
 Classical Magnet School
Richardson, Texas

Mary Leveron
Teacher
Velasco Elementary
Brazosport ISD
Freeport, Texas

Becky McClendon
Teacher
A.P. Beutel Elementary
Brazosport ISD
Freeport, Texas

Suzanne Milstead
Teacher
Liestman Elementary
Alief ISD
Houston, Texas

Debbie Oliver
Teacher
School Board of Broward County
Ft. Lauderdale, Florida

Sharon Pearthree
Teacher
School Board of Broward County
Ft. Lauderdale, Florida

Jayne Pedersen
Teacher
Laura B. Sprague School
District 103
Lincolnshire, Illinois

Sharon Pedroja
Teacher
Riverside Cultural
 Arts/History Magnet
Wichita Public Schools USD #259
Wichita, Kansas

Marcia Percell
Teacher
Pharr, San Juan, Alamo ISD
Pharr, Texas

Shirley Pfingston
Teacher
Orland School District #135
Orland Park, Illinois

Sharon S. Placko
Teacher
District 26, Mt. Prospect
Mt. Prospect, IL

Glenda Rall
Teacher
Seltzer Elementary
USD #259
Wichita, Kansas

Nelda Requenez
Teacher
Canterbury Elementary
Edinburg, Texas

Dr. Beth Rice
Teacher
Loxahatchee Groves
 Elementary School
Loxahatchee, Florida

Martha Salom Romero
Teacher
El Paso ISD
El Paso, Texas

Paula Sanders
Teacher
Welleby Elementary School
Sunrise, Florida

Lynn Setchell
Teacher
Sigsbee Elementary School
Key West, Florida

Rhonda Shook
Teacher
Mueller Elementary
Wichita Public Schools USD #259
Wichita, Kansas

Anna Marie Smith
Teacher
Orland School District #135
Orland Park, Illinois

Nancy Ann Varneke
Teacher
Seltzer Elementary
Wichita Public Schools USD #259
Wichita, Kansas

Aimee Walsh
Teacher
Rolling Meadows, Illinois

Ilene Wagner
Teacher
O.A. Thorp Scholastic Acacemy
Chicago Public Schools
Chicago, Illinois

Brian Warren
Teacher
Riley Community Consolidated
 School District 18
Marengo, Illinois

Tammie White
Teacher
Holley-Navarre
 Intermediate School
Navarre, Florida

Dr. Mychael Willon
Principal
Horace Mann Elementary
Wichita Public Schools
Wichita, Kansas

Inclusion Consultants

Dr. Eric J. Pyle, Ph.D.
Assistant Professor, Science Education
Department of Educational Theory
 and Practice
West Virginia University
Morgantown, West Virginia

Dr. Gretchen Butera, Ph.D.
Associate Professor, Special Education
Department of Education Theory
 and Practice
West Virginia University
Morgantown, West Virginia

Bilingual Consultant

Irma Gomez-Torres
Dalindo Elementary
Austin ISD
Austin, Texas

Bilingual Reviewers

Mary E. Morales
E.A. Jones Elementary
Fort Bend ISD
Missouri City, Texas

Gabriela T. Nolasco
Pebble Hills Elementary
Ysleta ISD
El Paso, Texas

Maribel B. Tanguma
Reed and Mock Elementary
San Juan, Texas

Yesenia Garza
Reed and Mock Elementary
San Juan, Texas

Teri Gallegos
St. Andrew's School
Austin, Texas

Using Scientific Methods
for Science Inquiry — xii

Using Process Skills
for Science Inquiry — xiv

❓ Science Inquiry — xvi

Unit A
Life Science

Science and Technology — A2

Chapter 1
Plant Structure and Function — A4

Explore Activity
Classifying Seeds — A6

Reading for Science
Identifying the Main Idea — A7

Lesson 1
How Are Plants Grouped? — A8

Lesson 2
What Are the Parts of a Flower? — A15

Lesson 3
How Do Flowers Make Seeds and Fruits? — A19

Investigate Activity
Observing the Parts of Flowers — A24

Lesson 4
What Is the Life Cycle of a Flowering Plant? — A26

Experiment Activity
Experimenting with Seed Germination — A29

Chapter Review — A32

Chapter 2
Animal Structure and Function — A34

Explore Activity
Exploring Animal Characteristics — A36

Math in Science
Making Bar Graphs — A37

Lesson 1
How Are Animals Alike and Different? — A38

Investigate Activity
Classifying Animals Without Backbones — A44

Lesson 2
How Do Animals with Backbones Vary? — A46

Lesson 3
What Characteristics Do Animals Get from Their Parents? — A54

Investigate Activity
Observing How Animals Respond to Stimuli — A60

Chapter Review — A62

Go to HUMAN BODY UNIT D Table of Contents

Chapter 3
Energy in Ecosystems — A 64

Explore Activity
Making a Woodland Habitat Model — A 66

Reading for Science
Using Context Clues — A 67

Lesson 1
What Is an Ecosystem? — A 68

Investigate Activity
Investigating a Habitat — A 72

Lesson 2
How Do Plants Get Energy? — A 74

Lesson 3
How Do Other Living Things Get Energy? — A 77

Lesson 4
What Are Food Chains and Food Webs? — A 82

Investigate Activity
Investigating Decomposition — A 90

Chapter Review — A 92

Chapter 4
Surviving in the Environment — A 94

Explore Activity
Exploring How Animals Hide — A 96

Math in Science
Solving Word Problems — A 97

Lesson 1
What Structures Help Plants and Animals Survive? — A 98

Lesson 2
What Behaviors Help Animals Survive? — A 105

Investigate Activity
Investigating Migration — A 112

Lesson 3
How Do Changes in the Environment Affect Survival? — A 114

Lesson 4
Do All Plants and Animals Survive? — A 118

Chapter Review — A 122

Unit A Review — A 124
Unit A Performance Review — A 126
Writing for Science — A 128

v

Unit B
Physical Science

Science and Technology	**B2**

Chapter 1
Measuring Matter — B4

Explore Activity
Exploring Matter — B6

Math in Science
Exploring Mass — B7

Lesson 1
What Is Matter? — B8

Lesson 2
How Are Length and Volume Measured? — B12

Lesson 3
How Do You Find Mass and Density? — B16

Investigate Activity
Describing and Measuring Matter — B20

Lesson 4
What Are Physical Changes? — B22

Lesson 5
What Are Chemical Changes? — B26

Chapter Review — B30

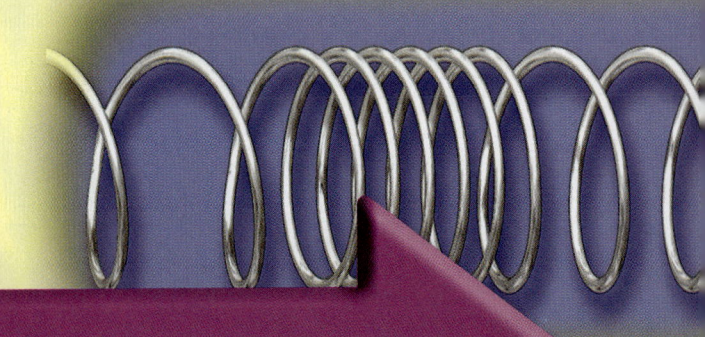

Go to HUMAN BODY UNIT D Table of Contents

Chapter 2
Force and Motion — B32

Explore Activity
Exploring Changes in Motion — B34

Math in Science
Exploring Weight — B35

Lesson 1
How Do Forces Affect Motion? — B36

Investigate Activity
Reducing Friction — B40

Lesson 2
How Does Energy Affect Motion? — B42

Investigate Activity
Changing Forms of Energy — B46

Lesson 3
How Are Work and Motion Related? — B48

Experiment Activity
Experimenting with Pulleys — B55

Chapter Review — B58

vi

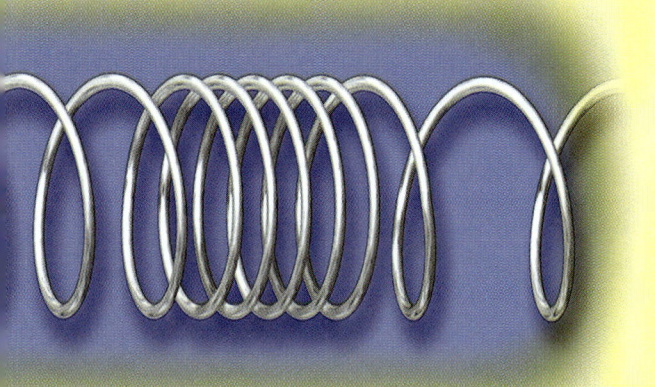

Chapter 3
Electricity and Magnetism — B 60

Explore Activity
Exploring Electric Charge — B 62

Reading for Science
Identifying Cause and Effect — B 63

Lesson 1
What Is an Electric Current? — B 64

Lesson 2
How Do Electric Circuits Work? — B 68

Investigate Activity
Comparing Series and Parallel Circuits — B 72

Lesson 3
What Is Magnetism? — B 74

Investigate Activity
Making an Electromagnet — B 78

Lesson 4
How Do Electricity and Magnetism Work Together? — B 80

Experiment Activity
Experimenting with Electromagnets — B 85

Chapter Review — B 88

Chapter 4
Light and Sound — B 90

Explore Activity
Exploring Colors in Light — B 92

Reading for Science
Using Graphic Sources — B 93

Lesson 1
What Is Light? — B 94

Lesson 2
What Happens When Light Hits an Object? — B 98

Investigate Activity
Observing Light Through Different Materials — B 104

Lesson 3
How Does Sound Travel? — B 106

Investigate Activity
Classifying Sounds — B 114

Lesson 4
How Do You Hear Sound? — B 116

Chapter Review — B 122

Unit B Review — B 124
Unit B Performance Review — B 126
Writing for Science — B 128

Unit C
Earth Science

Science and Technology	C2

Chapter 1
Measuring Weather — C4

Explore Activity
Exploring Surface Temperatures — C6

Math in Science
Exploring Range, Median, and Mode — C7

Lesson 1
How Does Sunlight Affect Air Temperature? — C8

Lesson 2
How Does Temperature Affect Air Movement? — C12

Lesson 3
What Causes Clouds and Precipitation? — C17

Investigate Activity
Investigating Air Pressure and Weather — C24

Lesson 4
How Do Meteorologists Predict Weather? — C26

Chapter Review — C32

Chapter 2
The Makeup of the Earth — C34

Explore Activity
Exploring How Magma Moves — C36

Reading for Science
Supporting Facts and Details — C37

Lesson 1
What Is the Earth's Surface Like? — C38

Lesson 2
How Do Weathering and Erosion Affect the Earth's Features? — C44

Lesson 3
What Materials Make Up the Earth's Features? — C48

Investigate Activity
Classifying Rocks — C54

Lesson 4
What Resources Are Found on the Earth? — C56

Chapter Review — C60

viii

Chapter 3
Exploring the Oceans — C62

Explore Activity
Measuring What You Can't See — C64

Math in Science
Using Logical Reasoning — C65

Lesson 1
How Do People Map the Ocean Floor? — C66

Lesson 2
How Can Scientists Explore the Ocean Depths? — C70

Investigate Activity
Investigating Currents and Waves — C76

Lesson 3
How Does Ocean Water Move? — C78

Lesson 4
Where Do Organisms Live in the Ocean? — C84

Experiment Activity
Experimenting with Brine Shrimp — C89

Chapter Review — C92

Chapter 4
Movements in the Solar System — C94

Explore Activity
Exploring Seasons — C96

Reading for Science
Making Predictions — C97

Lesson 1
What Are the Effects of Earth's Movements? — C98

Lesson 2
What Are the Effects of the Moon's Movements? — C102

Investigate Activity
Modeling the Phases of the Moon — C106

Lesson 3
How Does Earth Compare with Other Planets? — C108

Lesson 4
What Have Scientists Learned About Distant Planets? — C114

Lesson 5
What Other Objects Are Seen in the Solar System? — C118

Chapter Review — C122

Unit C Review — C124
Unit C Performance Review — C126
Writing for Science — C128

Go to HUMAN BODY UNIT D Table of Contents

ix

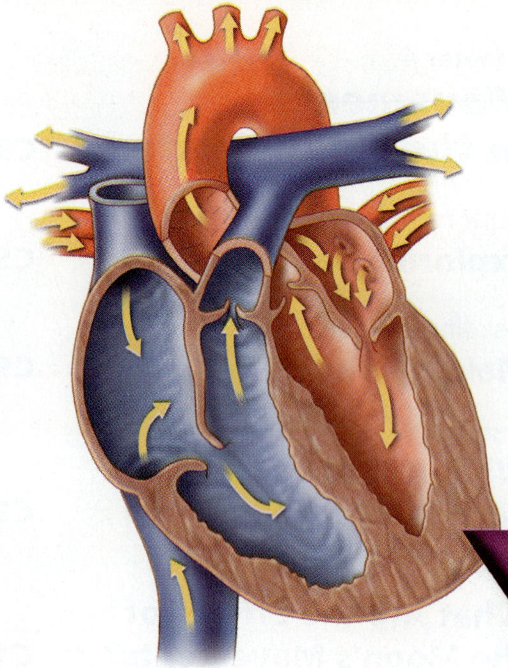

Here is the Table of Contents

Unit D
Human Body

Science and Technology D2

Chapter 1
The Digestive, Circulatory, and Nervous Systems D4

Explore Activity
Exploring Teeth D6

Math in Science
Exploring Capacity D7

Lesson 1
How Does the Digestive System Work? D8

Lesson 2
How Does the Circulatory System Work? D13

Investigate Activity
Investigating the Sense of Touch D18

Lesson 3
How Does the Brain Get Information? D20

Experiment Activity
Experimenting with the Sense of Smell D27

Chapter Review D30

Chapter 2
Keeping Your Body Systems Healthy — D 32

Explore Activity
Exploring Food Labels — D 34

Reading for Science
Identifying Cause and Effect — D 35

Lesson 1
How Can You Keep Your Digestive System Healthy? — D 36

Lesson 2
How Can You Keep Your Circulatory System Healthy? — D 40

Investigate Activity
Investigating How the Heart Works — D 46

Lesson 3
How Can You Keep Your Nervous System Healthy? — D 48

Investigate Activity
Conducting a Safety Survey — D 56

Chapter Review — D 58

Unit D Review — D 60
Unit D Performance Review — D 62
Writing for Science — D 64

Your Science Handbook

Table of Contents — 1
⚠ Safety in Science — 2
Using the Metric System — 4

Science Process Skills Lessons
  Observing — 6
  Communicating — 8
  Classifying — 10
  Estimating and Measuring — 12
  Inferring — 14
  Predicting — 16
  Making Operational Definitions — 18
  Making and Using Models — 20
  Formulating Questions and Hypotheses — 22
  Collecting and Interpreting Data — 24
  Identifying and Controlling Variables — 26
  Experimenting — 28

Science Reference Section — 30

Ⓗ **History of Science** — 48

Glossary — 60

Index — 70

xi

Using Scientific Methods for Science Inquiry

Scientists try to solve many problems. Scientists study problems in different ways, but they all use scientific methods to guide their work. Scientific methods are organized ways of finding answers and solving problems. Scientific methods include the steps shown on these pages. The order of the steps or the number of steps used may change. You can use these steps to organize your own scientific inquiries.

Which clay boat design holds more marbles before sinking?

State the Problem

The problem is the question you want to answer. Curiosity and inquiry have resulted in many scientific discoveries. State your problem in the form of a question.

Formulate Your Hypothesis

Your hypothesis is a possible answer to your problem. Make sure your hypothesis can be tested. Your hypothesis should take the form of a statement.

◀ A wide boat with high sides holds more marbles.

Identify and Control the Variables

For a fair test, you must select which variable to change and which variables to control. Choose one variable to change when you test your hypothesis. Control the other variables so they do not change.

▲ Make one boat wide and the other boat narrow. Both boats will have high sides. Use the same amount of clay for each boat.

Test Your Hypothesis

Do experiments to test your hypothesis. You may need to repeat experiments to make sure your results remain consistent. Sometimes you conduct a scientific survey to test a hypothesis.

◀ Place marbles in the boat until it sinks. Repeat for the other boat.

Collect Your Data

As you test your hypothesis, you will collect data about the problem you want to solve. You may need to record measurements. You might make drawings or diagrams. Or you may write lists or descriptions. Collect as much data as you can while testing your hypothesis.

Interpret Your Data

By organizing your data into charts, tables, diagrams, and graphs, you may see patterns in the data. Then you can decide what the information from your data means.

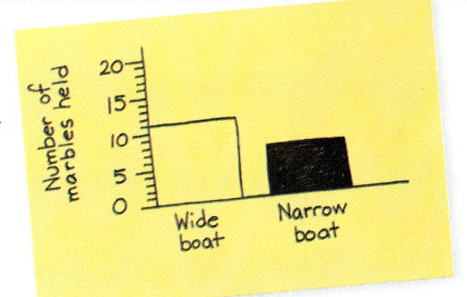

State Your Conclusion

Your conclusion is a decision you make based on evidence. Compare your results with your hypothesis. Based on whether or not your data supports your hypothesis, decide if your hypothesis is correct or incorrect. Then communicate your conclusion by stating or presenting your decision.

A wide boat design holds more marbles!

❓ Inquire Further

Use what you learn to solve other problems or to answer other questions that you might have. You may decide to repeat your experiment, or to change it based on what you learned.

▼ Will the results be similar with aluminum foil boats?

xiii

Using Process Skills for Science Inquiry

These 12 process skills are used by scientists when they do their research. You also use many of these skills every day. For example, when you think of a statement that you can test, you are using process skills. When you gather data to make a chart or graph, you are using process skills. As you do the activities in your book, you will use these same process skills.

I see..., I smell..., I hear..., It feels like..., I never taste without permission!

Observing
Use one or more of your senses—seeing, hearing, smelling, touching, or tasting—to gather information about objects or events.

Communicating
Share information about what you learn using words, pictures, charts, graphs, and diagrams.

Classifying
Arrange or group objects according to their common properties.

◀ Rocks with one color in Group 1.

Rocks with two or more colors in Group 2. ▶

Estimating and Measuring
Make an estimate about an object's properties, then measure and describe the object in units.

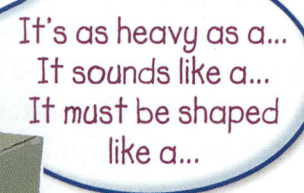

Inferring
Draw a conclusion or make a reasonable guess based on what you observe, or from your past experiences.

It's as heavy as a... It sounds like a... It must be shaped like a...

Predicting
Form an idea about what will happen based on evidence.

◀ Predict what happens after 15 minutes.

Making Operational Definitions
Define or describe an object or event based on your experiences with it.

An electromagnet is a coil of wire around a bolt that... ▶

Making and Using Models
Make real or mental representations to explain ideas, objects, or events.

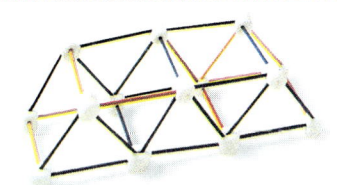

◀ It's different from a real bridge because... The model is like a real bridge because...

If you place a plant by a sunny window, the leaves will... ▶

Formulating Questions and Hypotheses
Think of a statement that you can test to solve a problem or to answer a question about how something works.

Collecting and Interpreting Data
Gather observations and measurements into graphs, tables, charts, or diagrams. Then use the information to solve problems or answer questions.

The plant in the polluted water grew the slowest.

Identifying and Controlling Variables
Change one factor that may affect the outcome of an event while holding other factors constant.

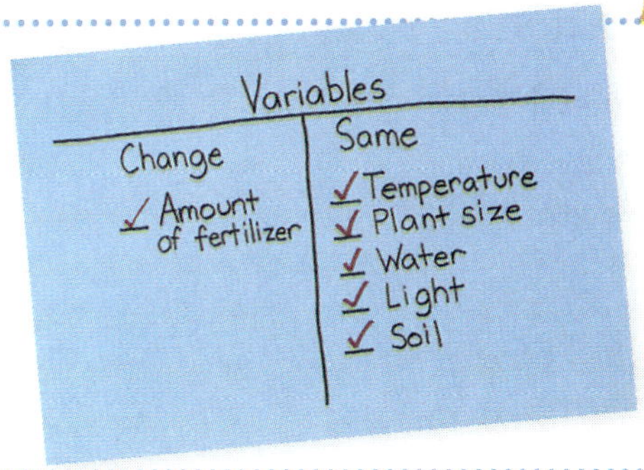

Experimenting
Design an investigation to test a hypothesis or to solve a problem. Then form a conclusion.

I'll write a clear procedure so that other students could repeat the experiment.

Science Inquiry

Throughout your science book, you will ask questions, do investigations, answer your questions, and tell others what you have learned. Use the descriptions below to help you during your scientific inquiry.

What kind of cup keeps liquid colder?

1 **Ask a question about objects, organisms, and events in the environment.**

You will find the answer to your question from your own observations and investigations and from reliable sources of scientific information.

2 **Plan and conduct a simple investigation.**

The kind of investigation you do depends on the question you ask. Kinds of investigations include describing objects, events, and organisms; classifying them; and doing a fair test or experiment.

3 **Use simple equipment and tools to gather data and extend the senses.**

Equipment and tools you might use include rulers and meter sticks, compasses, thermometers, watches, balances, spring scales, hand lenses, microscopes, cameras, calculators, and computers.

4 **Use data to construct a reasonable explanation.**

Use the information that you have gathered to answer your question and support your answer. Compare your answer to scientific knowledge, your experiences, and the observations of others.

5 **Communicate investigations and explanations.**

Share your work with others by writing, drawing, or talking. Describe your work in a way that others could repeat your investigation.

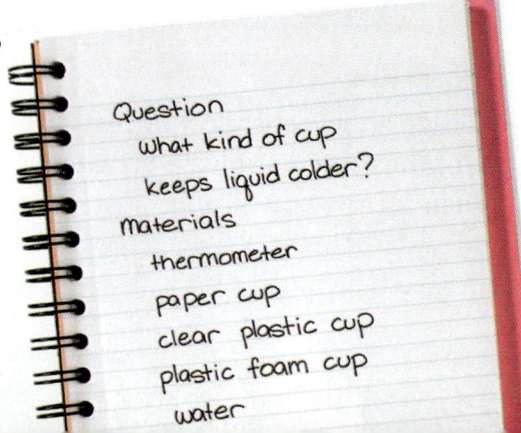

Question
What kind of cup keeps liquid colder?
materials
thermometer
paper cup
clear plastic cup
plastic foam cup
water

xvi

Human Body

Chapter 1
The Digestive, Circulatory, and Nervous Systems — D 4

Chapter 2
Keeping Your Body Systems Healthy — D 32

Your Science Handbook

Table of Contents	1
Safety in Science	2
Using the Metric System	4
Science Process Skills Lessons	6
Science Reference Section	30
History of Science	48
Glossary	60
Index	70

Science and Technology
In Your World!

Computers Get Smarter and Smarter!

Today's computers can do millions—even billions—of calculations in the blink of an eye. But they can't think and learn as humans do. Some scientists want to change that, and they've made amazing progress! For example, a supercomputer named Deep Blue defeated the world's chess champion in 1997. Until then, most people believed that playing championship chess required human intelligence. You will learn about the brain in **Chapter 1 The Digestive, Circulatory, and Nervous Systems.**

Preservation Methods Keep Food from Turning Yucky!

People use many methods to keep food from spoiling, including canning, freezing, and freeze-drying. Now technology has given us aseptic packaging. In this method, solid or liquid food is heated to a high temperature to kill germs, and then put in germ-free containers. Juice and milk in foil-lined cardboard boxes are popular examples. They're easy to carry, and they can be stored outside a refrigerator for months. You will learn more about food safety in **Chapter 2 Keeping Your Body Systems Healthy.**

Your Amazing Heart!

Just think! Your heart never stops beating. It keeps on beating without your even having to think about it. When you jog, your heart speeds up to carry oxygen to your muscles so you can run.

D4

Chapter 1
The Digestive, Circulatory, and Nervous Systems

Inquiring about The Digestive, Circulatory, and Nervous Systems

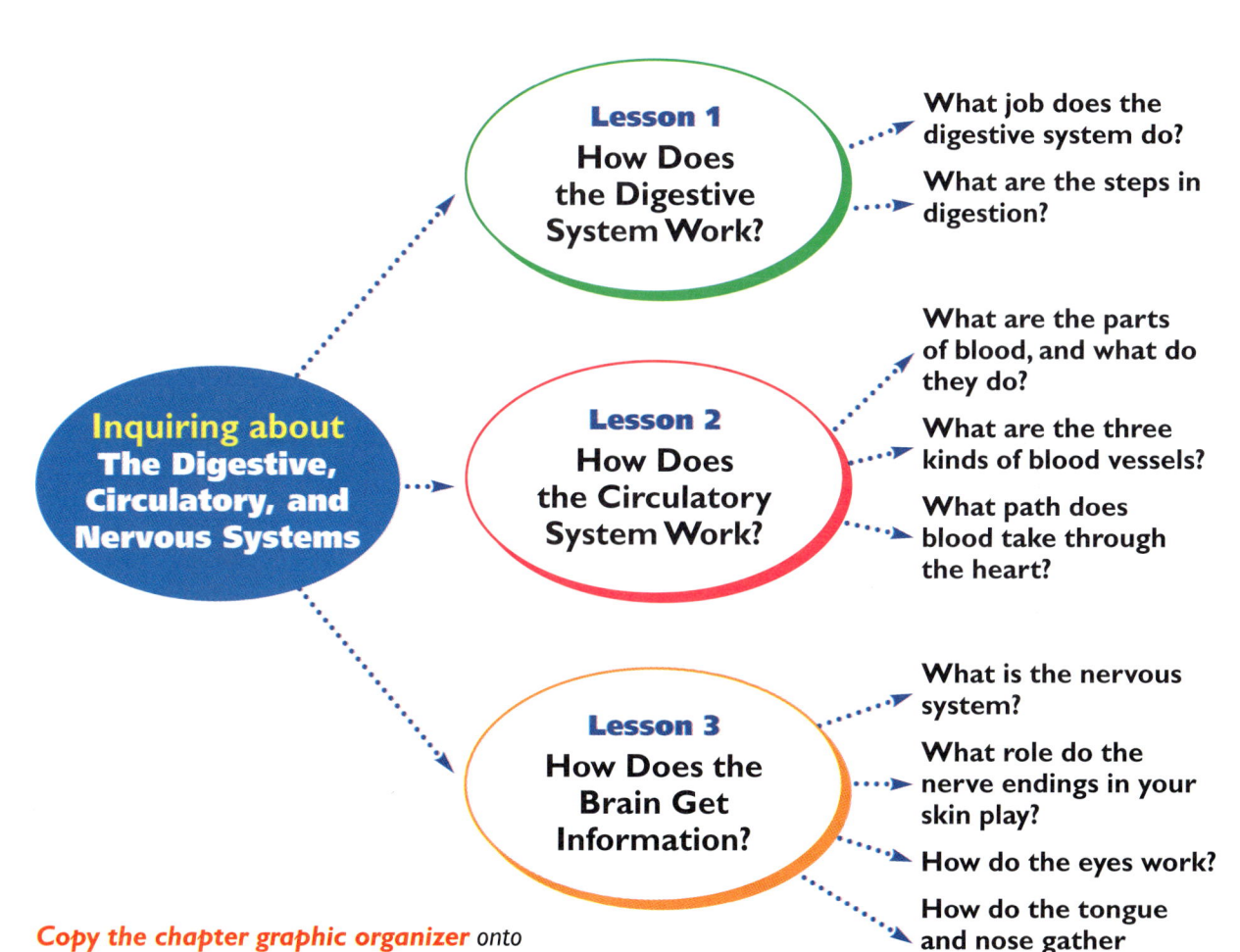

- **Lesson 1: How Does the Digestive System Work?**
  - What job does the digestive system do?
  - What are the steps in digestion?

- **Lesson 2: How Does the Circulatory System Work?**
  - What are the parts of blood, and what do they do?
  - What are the three kinds of blood vessels?
  - What path does blood take through the heart?

- **Lesson 3: How Does the Brain Get Information?**
  - What is the nervous system?
  - What role do the nerve endings in your skin play?
  - How do the eyes work?
  - How do the tongue and nose gather information?

Copy the chapter graphic organizer onto your own paper. This organizer shows you what the whole chapter is all about. As you read the lessons and do the activities, look for answers to the questions and write them on your organizer.

D5

Explore Activity

Exploring Teeth

Process Skills
- observing
- classifying
- communicating
- inferring

Materials
- plastic mirror

Explore

① Use a mirror to **observe** the fronts of all your teeth. Then observe the chewing surfaces of your lower teeth by opening your mouth and tipping the mirror until you get a good view. Then observe the chewing surfaces of your upper teeth.

② Make a drawing of your lower and upper teeth to record your observations.

③ **Classify** your teeth by shape. Write a phrase describing each kind of tooth shape you observed. You should have three or four phrases.

Reflect

1. **Communicate.** Discuss the descriptions of your teeth with your classmates.

2. Make an **inference.** Which teeth do you think would be best to take a bite of an apple? Which teeth would be best for chewing and grinding the apple? Explain.

Inquire Further

What do teeth with different shapes do to different kinds of food, such as a celery stick, meat, or popcorn? Develop a plan to answer this or other questions you may have.

Math in Science

Exploring Capacity

Liters (L) and **milliliters** (mL) are metric units of **capacity**. In math, capacity is the amount a container can hold. An Olympic-size swimming pool has a capacity of about 500,000 **liters** of water. Your heart pumps the equivalent of 7,500 liters of blood every day of your life.

Work Together

Use estimation and measurement to explore metric capacity.

1. Find the capacity of the spoon.
   a. Estimate how many milliliters of water will fit in the spoon.
   b. Fill the spoon with water and pour it into the measuring cup.
   c. Count the number of spoonfuls that will fill the measuring cup to the 25 mL mark.
   d. Divide 25 mL by the number of spoonfuls. This is the capacity of the spoon.

2. Find the capacity of the mug.
   a. Fill the measuring cup to 100 mL.
   b. Estimate how many milliliters will fit in the mug. Check.

3. Find how many milliliters are in a liter.
   a. Fill the measuring cup to 250 mL.
   b. Empty the water into the liter container. Estimate how many times it will take to fill 1 liter. Check.
   c. Multiply 250 mL by the number of times you poured. How many milliliters are in a liter?

Talk About It!

How did you find how many milliliters are in a liter?

Materials
- water
- plastic spoon
- metric measuring cup [250 mL]
- mug
- 1-liter container

Math Vocabulary

capacity, the amount a container can hold

liter, a unit for measuring capacity in the metric system

milliliter, $\frac{1}{1,000}$ of a liter

Did you know?

An average-sized man has about 4.8 to 6.6 liters of blood in his body at any one time. An average-sized woman has about 3.8 to 5.7 liters of blood.

What's the Big Idea?

You will learn:
- what job the digestive system does.
- what the steps in digestion are.

Glossary

nutrient (nü′trē ənt), a substance in food that the body uses for energy, for growth and repair, or for working well

digestion (də jes′chən), the changing of food into forms that the body can use

Lesson 1

How Does the Digestive System Work?

As you munch your favorite sandwich, your best friend comes up. "What's going on?" she asks. "Just feeding the old cells," you say. "Yum," she says. "So, how do you know that your cells like peanut butter?"

What the Digestive System Does

Of course, the cells that make up your body don't like or dislike particular foods. However, cells do need food's nourishing substances to stay alive and do their work. These substances are called **nutrients**.

Some nutrients give you the energy you need to play and do all the other things you do each day. Some nutrients help you grow, because body cells use the nutrients to make new cells. Your body also uses nutrients to make repairs, such as mending a broken bone. Certain nutrients help your body work as it should.

Any food you eat must be changed into nutrients that your cells can use. Your digestive system does this job, which is called **digestion**.

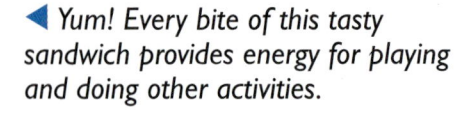

◀ Yum! Every bite of this tasty sandwich provides energy for playing and doing other activities.

Steps in Digestion

Digestion begins as soon as you bite into food. For example, as you chew a sandwich, your teeth cut and grind the bread and the filling into smaller pieces. Your tongue helps mix the chewed food with **saliva**, the liquid in your mouth. Saliva makes the food wet and easy to swallow.

Saliva also contains an **enzyme**, or chemical, that helps break food down so saliva can change the food into nutrients. The enzyme in saliva helps change starches into sugars. That is why you may notice a sweet taste when you chew bread, crackers, and other starchy foods.

When you have finished chewing, your tongue moves the wet lump of food to the back of your mouth. You swallow, and the food enters a tube called the **esophagus**. Your bite of sandwich is now on its way to the next stop in the digestive system—your stomach.

Glossary

saliva (sə lī′və), the liquid in the mouth that makes chewed food wet and begins digestion

enzyme (en′zīm), a chemical that helps your digestive system change food into nutrients

esophagus (i sof′ə gəs), the tube that carries food and liquids from the mouth to the stomach

The starches in sandwich bread are made of sugars joined together. Saliva changes the starches into sugars. ▼

Glossary

small intestine
(in tes′tən), the organ of the digestive system in which most digestion takes place

The Digestive System

The picture and captions on these two pages show what happens as food moves through the parts of the digestive system. As you read, use your finger to trace the path that food takes.

1 Mouth
As teeth tear, cut, and grind food, three pairs of glands make saliva. These salivary glands are located in front of the ears, under the lower jaw, and under the tongue. Tiny tubes carry the saliva from the salivary glands to the mouth.

2 Esophagus
The esophagus of an adult is about 25 centimeters long. Muscles in the esophagus contract and relax to push swallowed food down toward the stomach. The process is something like squeezing toothpaste out of a tube.

3 Stomach
The stomach is a baglike organ with muscular walls. Stomach muscles squeeze and mix food with digestive juice made in the stomach's lining. The juice changes the food, which stays in the stomach for two to four hours. When the food leaves the stomach, it is a thick liquid.

4 Small Intestine
The liquid food is pushed into the **small intestine**, a curled-up tube. If stretched out, an adult's small intestine would be about 7 meters long. Most digestion takes place in the three to six hours that food stays in the small intestine. Juices made in the lining of the small intestine and other organs mix with food. The juices change the food into nutrients. The nutrients pass through the thin walls of blood vessels in the intestinal lining. Blood carries the nutrients to body cells.

5 Large Intestine
The parts of food that cannot be digested move to the large intestine, along with some liquid. The large intestine removes much of the liquid and stores the resulting solid waste until it leaves the body. Read more about the large intestine on page D12.

D11

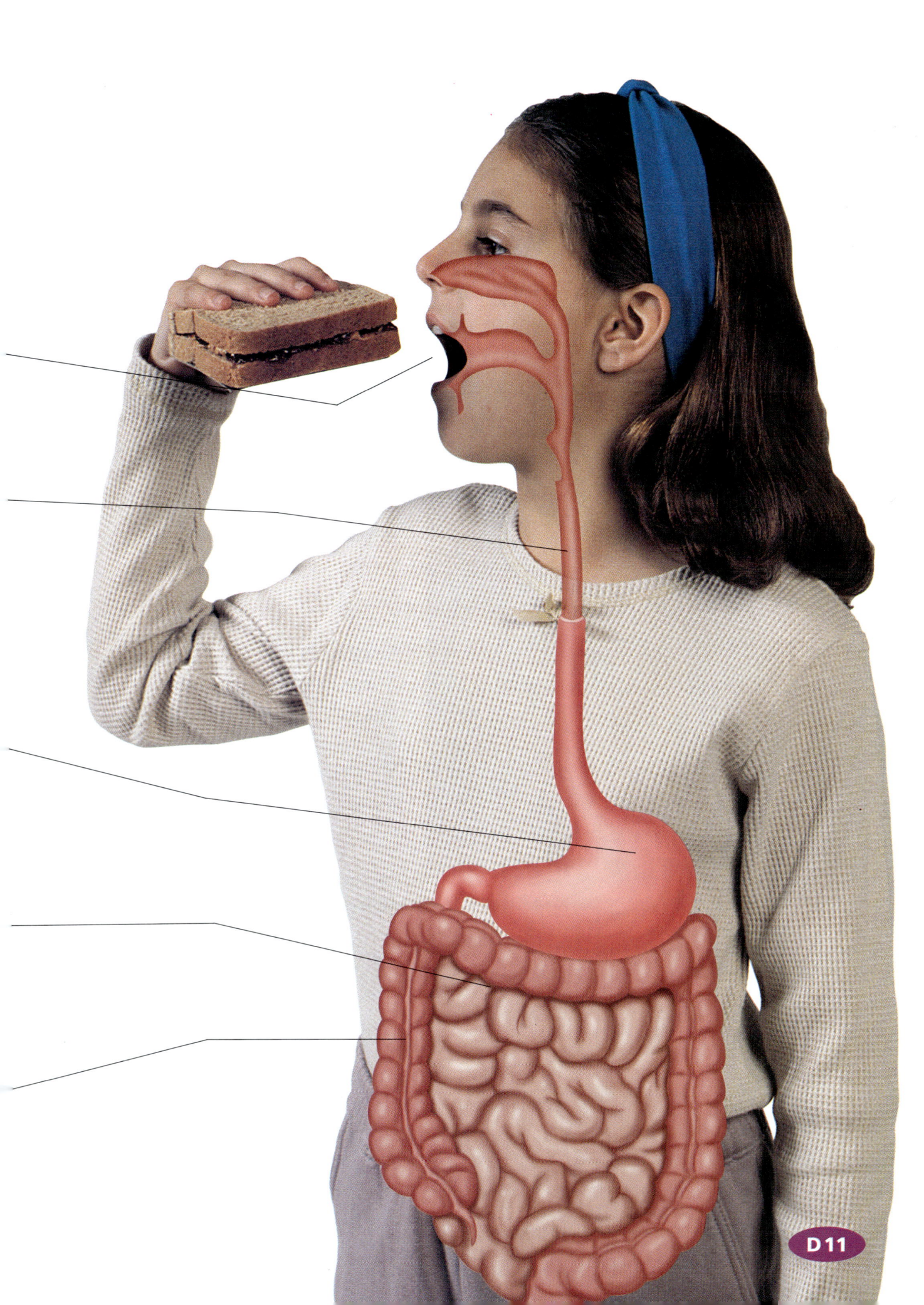

You saw that the digestive system includes two intestines. Like the small intestine, the large intestine is a curled-up tube. Its name comes from the fact that it is more than twice as wide as the small intestine. However, the large intestine is only about one and a half meters long in an adult.

Not everything in food can be broken down into parts that the body can use. For example, the skins and seeds of fruits and vegetables cannot be digested. Undigested food, along with liquid left over from digestive juices, moves from the small intestine to the large intestine.

The large intestine removes much of the water from the mixture. The water is drawn through the thin walls of the large intestine into the blood. What is left in the large intestine is called solid waste. The X ray shows a large intestine with solid waste in it. Solid waste leaves the body after ten hours to a day or more in the large intestine.

▲ *In this X ray, the backbone and hips look greenish-yellow in the background. The tube is the large intestine. Notice the brightly colored waste in the large intestine.*

Lesson 1 Review

1. How does the digestive system help body cells?
2. What happens to food in the stomach?
3. **Capacity**
   Your stomach produces about 2 liters of acid that helps digest food each day. How many milliliters of acid does your stomach produce?

Lesson 2

How Does the Circulatory System Work?

Put your hand on your chest. You can feel the steady **THUMP, THUMP** of your heart. In just one minute, your heart beats about ninety times, pumping blood all the way to the tips of your toes and back again.

Parts of Blood

Your heart, your blood, and the tubes that carry blood make up your circulatory system. This system takes nutrients, oxygen, and water to all your body cells. The system picks up wastes made by cells and carries the wastes to organs that get rid of them. Your circulatory system also helps keep you well.

Plasma is the watery part of blood. Nutrients, wastes, and blood cells float in plasma. Blood gets its color from **red blood cells**, shown in the picture. Red blood cells carry oxygen.

White blood cells protect you from sickness. Some white blood cells surround and destroy germs. Others make chemicals that kill germs. **Platelets** are tiny parts of cells. When you get a cut, platelets help stop the bleeding.

What's the Big Idea?

You will learn:
- what the parts of blood are and what they do.
- about the three kinds of blood vessels.
- what the path of blood through your heart is.

Glossary

plasma (plaz′mə), the watery part of blood that carries nutrients, wastes, and blood cells

red blood cell, the kind of blood cell that carries oxygen to other body cells

white blood cell, the kind of blood cell that fights germs

platelet (plāt′lit), a tiny part of a cell that helps stop bleeding

- Red blood cell
- One kind of white blood cell
- Platelet

D 13

Glossary

artery (är′tər ē), the kind of blood vessel that carries blood away from the heart

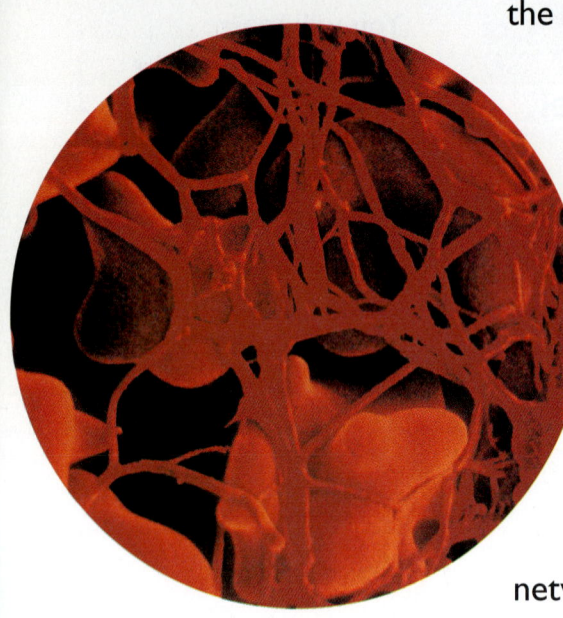

▲ Platelets, sticky fibers, and trapped blood cells clump together to form a clot.

When a blood vessel in the skin is cut, some blood leaks out. However, platelets soon clump together at the break in the blood vessel. The platelets give off a substance that causes a tangle of sticky fibers to form. Platelets, fibers, and trapped blood cells clump together to form a clot, as shown in the picture. The clot seals the break in the blood vessel. The bleeding stops.

After a while, the clot hardens to form a scab. The scab helps keep germs out of the cut. If germs do get in, white blood cells attack them. If there are a lot of germs, some white blood cells die in the attack. They form a thick, yellowish liquid called pus. Washing and bandaging a cut can help keep germs out while the cut heals.

Kinds of Blood Vessels

Most of the time, blood flows through a network of blood vessels. Your circulatory system has three kinds of blood vessels. Each kind does a different job.

An **artery** is a blood vessel that carries blood away from the heart. Find the arteries in the large picture on the next page. Notice that the large arteries connected to the heart branch into smaller and smaller arteries.

If you place the tips of your fingers on the inside of your wrist and press firmly, you can feel a beat. You are pressing on an artery. You feel the beat because the walls of arteries stretch as the heart pumps blood through them.

Blood in the smallest arteries flows into tiny blood vessels called **capillaries**, shown in the small picture below. Capillaries are so narrow that red blood cells go through them in single file. Capillaries have thin walls. Oxygen and nutrients carried by the blood pass through capillary walls into body cells. Wastes from body cells pass through capillary walls into the blood.

A **vein** is a blood vessel that carries blood from the capillaries back to the heart. Blood in the capillaries flows into tiny veins. These veins join together to make larger and larger veins. The blood in veins flows more slowly than the blood in arteries. To keep the blood from flowing backward, many veins have valves that work like one-way doors.

Glossary

capillary (kap′ə ler′ē), a tiny blood vessel with thin walls through which oxygen, nutrients, and wastes pass

vein (vān), the kind of blood vessel that carries blood back to the heart

Red blood cells move in single file through a capillary. ▼

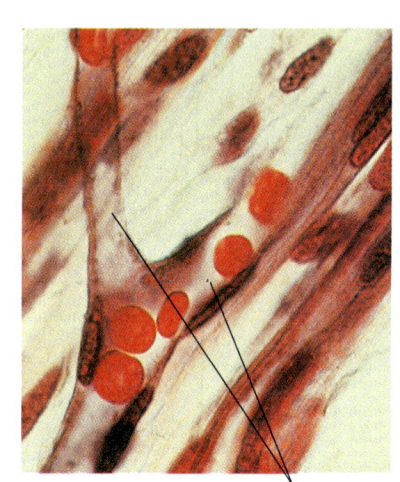

Capillaries

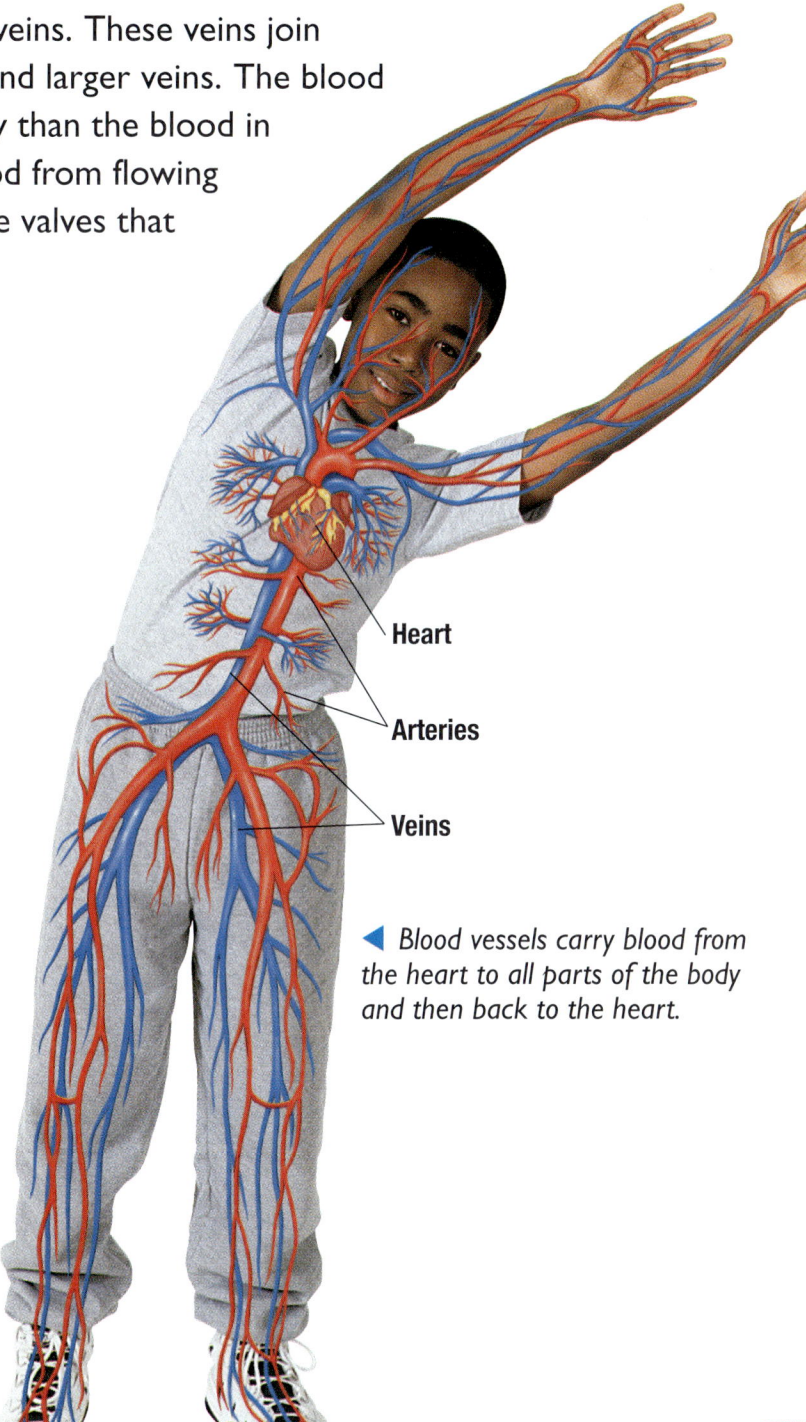

Heart

Arteries

Veins

◀ *Blood vessels carry blood from the heart to all parts of the body and then back to the heart.*

D 15

Glossary

atrium (ā′trē əm), one of two spaces in the top part of the heart that receive blood from veins

ventricle (ven′trə kəl), one of two spaces in the bottom part of the heart that pump blood out of the heart

The Path of Blood Through the Heart

Your heart is a hollow, muscular organ that pumps blood every minute of every day. The inside of the heart is divided into four spaces. Each **atrium** receives blood from veins. Each **ventricle** pumps blood out of the heart through arteries. As you read the next page, trace the path of blood in the picture below.

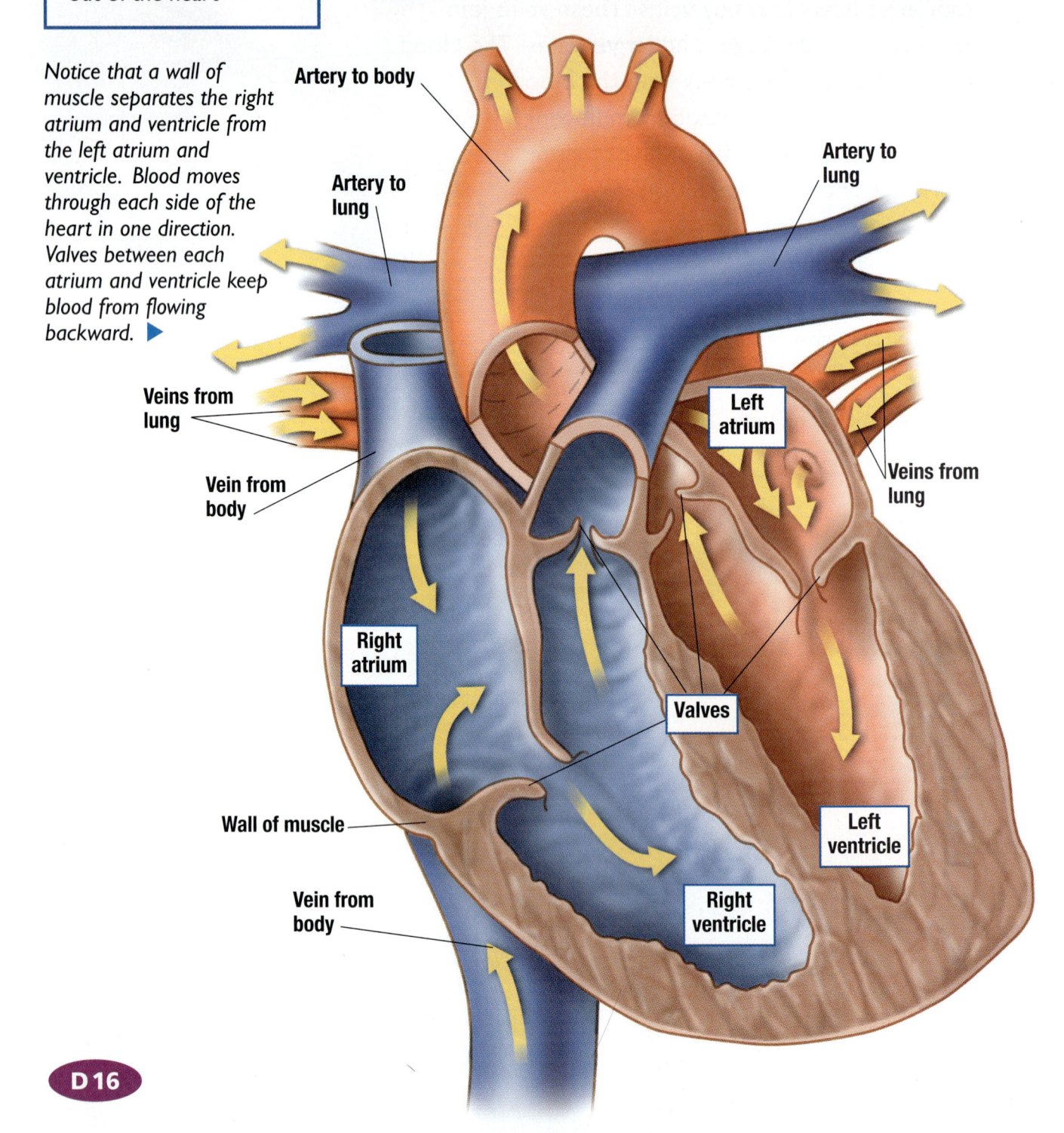

Notice that a wall of muscle separates the right atrium and ventricle from the left atrium and ventricle. Blood moves through each side of the heart in one direction. Valves between each atrium and ventricle keep blood from flowing backward. ▶

D 16

Find the two large veins from the body in the picture on page D16. These veins carry blood that has delivered oxygen to body cells. The oxygen-poor blood flows into the right atrium and then into the right ventricle. The right ventricle contracts, pumping the blood into a large artery. That artery divides into smaller arteries leading to the lungs. The blood picks up oxygen in the lungs.

Now find the veins that return oxygen-rich blood from the lungs to the heart. The blood flows into the left atrium and then into the left ventricle. The left ventricle contracts, pumping the blood into a large artery. That artery divides into smaller arteries leading to all parts of the body.

The two sides of the heart work in unison. For example, blood from the body enters the right atrium at the same time that blood from the lungs enters the left atrium. The right ventricle pumps blood to the lungs at the same time that the left ventricle pumps blood to all parts of the body.

Modern technology produced the special picture of a heart that you see on this page. Doctors use such pictures to decide whether a person's heart is working as it should.

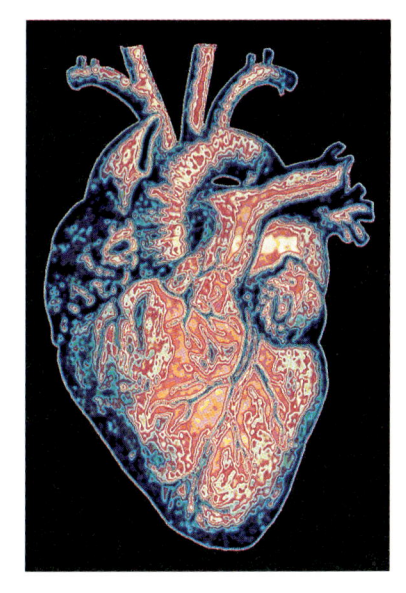

▲ *A computer image of the heart can show how well the heart is pumping blood.*

Lesson 2 Review

1. Name two parts of blood and their jobs.
2. What are the three kinds of blood vessels and what are their jobs?
3. Into which part of the heart does oxygen-poor blood flow?
4. **Graphic Sources**
   Use the picture on page D16 to make a graphic organizer showing how blood moves through the heart.

Investigate Activity

Investigating the Sense of Touch

Process Skills
- observing
- collecting and interpreting data
- inferring
- communicating

Materials
- safety goggles
- bobby pin
- metric ruler

Getting Ready
In this activity you will find out how the sense of touch varies.

Follow This Procedure

1 Make a chart like the one shown. Use your chart to record your observations.

	Felt 1 point when 1 point was used		Felt 2 points when 2 points were used	
	Yes	No	Yes	No
Neck				
Wrist				
Palm				
Finger				

2 Put on your safety goggles. Bend the bobby pin so the points are 5 mm apart (Photo A).

3 Lightly touch the back of another student's neck with either one or two points. Ask the student to **observe** how many points he or she feels. **Collect data** by making a mark in the appropriate place in your chart.

⚠️ **Safety Note** Be very gentle when touching skin with the bobby pin.

4 Repeat step 3 until you have tested five times with one point and five times with two points. Do the test in a random way, so there is no pattern that the other student might recognize.

Photo A

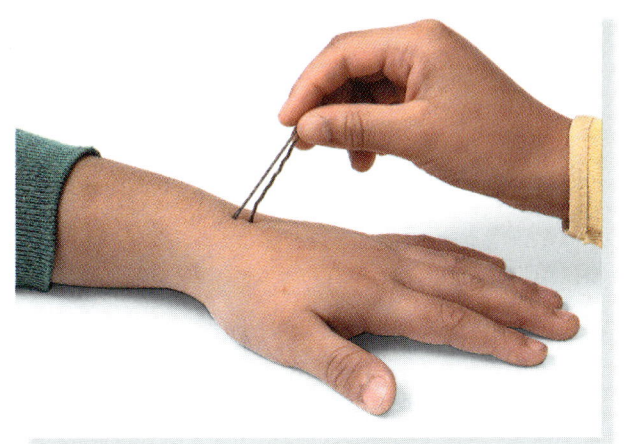

Photo B

5️⃣ Repeat the procedure on the back of a wrist (Photo B), on the palm of a hand, and on a fingertip. For each trial, have the student look away from you so he or she cannot see how many points are being tested.

Self-Monitoring
Have I correctly completed all the steps, including recording results in my chart?

Interpret Your Results

1. Find the total number of *Yes* answers for each body part. Then find the total number of *No* answers for each body part. For which body part did you record the highest number of *Yes* answers? the highest number of *No* answers?

2. Draw a conclusion. Which of the body parts tested were the most sensitive? the least sensitive?

3. Make an inference. What might be the advantage of having especially sensitive skin on some body parts that you tested? **Communicate** your ideas by writing a short paragraph.

❓ Inquire Further

What might happen if you tested other parts of the body, such as the upper arms, the calves of the legs, or the soles of the feet? Develop a plan to answer this or other questions you may have.

Self-Assessment

- I followed instructions to test another student's sense of touch.
- I **collected data** by recording my **observations** in a chart.
- I drew a conclusion about the sense of touch on different parts of the body.
- I made an **inference** about the advantages of having especially sensitive skin on some body parts that I tested.
- I **communicated** by writing about my inference.

What's the Big Idea?

You will learn:
- about the nervous system.
- what role the nerve endings in your skin play.
- how your eyes work.
- how your tongue and nose gather information.

Glossary

sense organ (sens ôr′gən), a body part that has special nerve cells that gather information about the surroundings

nerve cell (nėrv sel), a cell that gathers and carries information in the body

Lesson 3

How Does the Brain Get Information?

A friend has sent you a gift! It's in a sturdy box, so you can't tell what it is by squeezing or looking. You shake the box—gently at first, then harder. RATTLE, RATTLE! What can it be?

The Nervous System

You may be able to tell what the box holds just by listening. Chances are, though, you won't learn the secret until you look inside. Either way, you get information from your surroundings. Your brain decides what the information means and tells you what to do about it. Your brain and the other body parts that receive and send information make up your nervous system.

You notice your surroundings with your **sense organs**. Your ears, eyes, nose, tongue, and skin are sense organs. Each sense organ has special **nerve cells** that gather information from all around you.

See it! Hear it! Smell it! Taste it! Touch it! Your sense organs help you understand and enjoy the wonderful world around you. ▶

D20

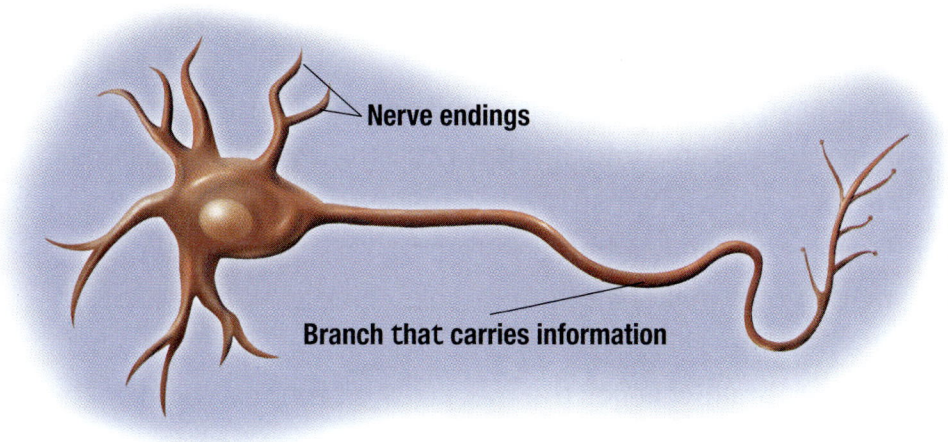

Nerve endings

Branch that carries information

◀ Nerve cells gather information and carry it to other nerve cells.

Nerve cells in the ears and eyes of the girl on page D20 gather information about sound and light. Nerve cells in the nose and tongue of the boy eating the apple gather information about scent and flavor. Skin has nerve cells that gather information about pressure, touch, pain, heat, and cold. What information might be gathered by the skin on the girl's hands as she holds her cat?

As you can see in the drawing above, nerve cells have a special shape. The tiny branches gather information from other nerve cells or from the outside world. These tiny branches are called **nerve endings**. The long branch of the nerve cell carries information to other nerve cells.

Glossary

nerve ending (nėrv en′ding), a tiny branch of a nerve cell that gathers information

Glossary

spinal cord
(spī′nl kôrd), a thick bundle of nerves that connects the brain and nerves throughout the body

Nerve cells are the basic units of your entire nervous system. Information gathered by nerve cells in your sense organs travels along nerves to your brain. A nerve is a bundle of nerve cells. Your brain is made up of millions of nerve cells. Find these parts of the nervous system on the next page.

Your brain changes the messages it receives so that you can understand them. Suppose your ears catch sound waves coming from the mouth of the kitten shown on the next page. The ears send messages about the sound waves to your brain. You don't actually hear a "meow" sound until your brain tells you so.

Messages from most parts of your body travel through your spinal cord. The **spinal cord** is a bundle of nerves that connects your brain with nerves throughout your body. You can't see it in the picture on the next page, but a long chain of bones encloses and protects the delicate spinal cord. This chain of bones is called the backbone, or spine.

Nerve Endings in Your Skin

Your skin has many nerve endings in it. Different nerve endings gather information about touch, pressure, heat, cold, and pain. Find the different kinds of nerve endings in the cross section of skin below.

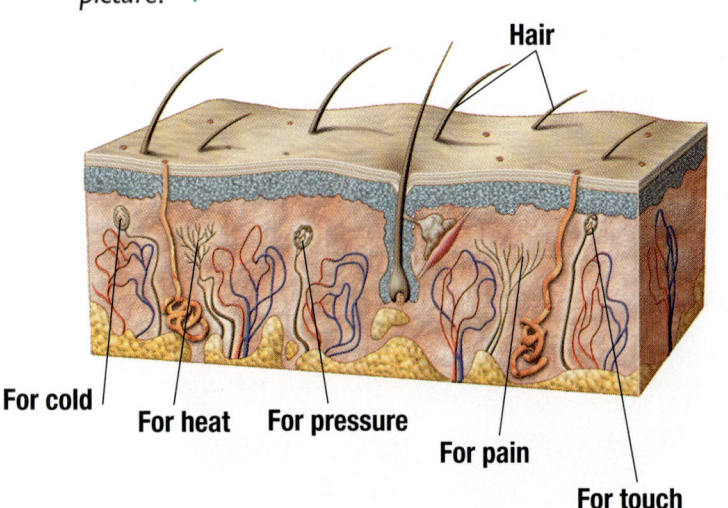

Nerve endings in the skin send messages to the brain, and the brain responds. For example, if someone lightly and repeatedly touches your bare foot, nerve endings for touch send a series of messages. The brain interprets the messages as tickling. The brain then sends messages that may cause you to laugh and try to pull away.

The different kinds of nerve endings are shown in the picture. ▼

Hair
For cold
For heat
For pressure
For pain
For touch

The Nervous System
Your nervous system controls all the activities that you think about, from reading a book to playing with a pet. Your nervous system also controls body activities that you do not have to think about. ▶

Brain
The brain is a soft, wrinkly organ. The bones of your skull help protect your brain from injury.

Spinal Cord
The spinal cord extends from your brain down the length of your back. If you run your finger down the center of your back, you can feel the bones that protect the spinal cord.

Nerves
Many nerves branch off from the spinal cord. They divide again and again, reaching every part of your body. Nerves thread their way through all your body organs.

D 23

▲ The clear covering at the front of the eye protects the eye and bends light. The eye is filled with a jellylike material that helps the eye keep its round shape.

How Your Eyes Work

Most information about your world comes to you through your sense of sight. You can see people, animals, books, and other things because light reflects off them. Some of this light travels to your eyes.

The outer parts of the eye show clearly in the picture below. You can see the iris, which is the colored part of the eye, and the black-looking pupil in the center of the iris. Now look at the drawing on the left. Notice that the pupil is actually a hole that lets light inside the eye. The iris is a ring of muscle that changes the pupil's size to let in the right amount of light. The pupil gets smaller in bright light and larger in dim light.

A clear lens lies behind the pupil. The lens bends light to focus it on the retina. The retina is a thin layer of nerve cells at the back of the eye. The nerve cells gather information about the light that strikes them. They send a message to the brain along a nerve called the optic nerve. Your brain interprets the message, and you know what you are seeing.

◀ The iris gives the eye its color. What color are your irises?

The Tongue and Nose

Like your skin and eyes, your tongue and nose give you information about your surroundings. Sometimes these sense organs help protect you. The smell of smoke can warn you of a fire. The bad smell and taste of certain spoiled foods can warn you not to eat them. Mostly, though, your tongue and nose help you enjoy the tastes and smells of your world.

Your sense of taste comes from tiny taste buds on your tongue. The taste buds are grouped around the bases of the small bumps that you have on your tongue. Find those bumps in the enlarged picture on the right.

Taste buds have nerve cells that gather information about four tastes. The tastes are sweet, sour, salty, and bitter. All the flavors you know are combinations of those tastes. For example, when you eat an orange, taste buds for sweet and sour send messages to your brain. Your brain interprets the messages. As you can see in the labeled photograph, each kind of taste bud is located on a different part of the tongue.

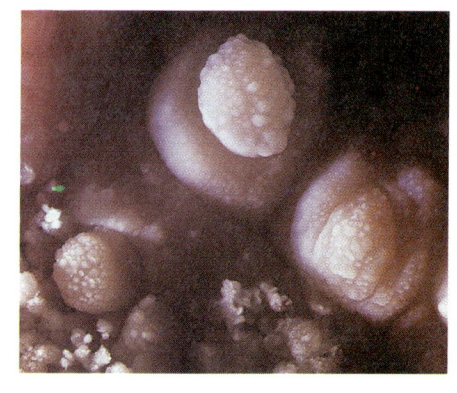

▲ This section of the tongue has been enlarged eight times. Even so, you can't see the tiny taste buds clustered around each bump.

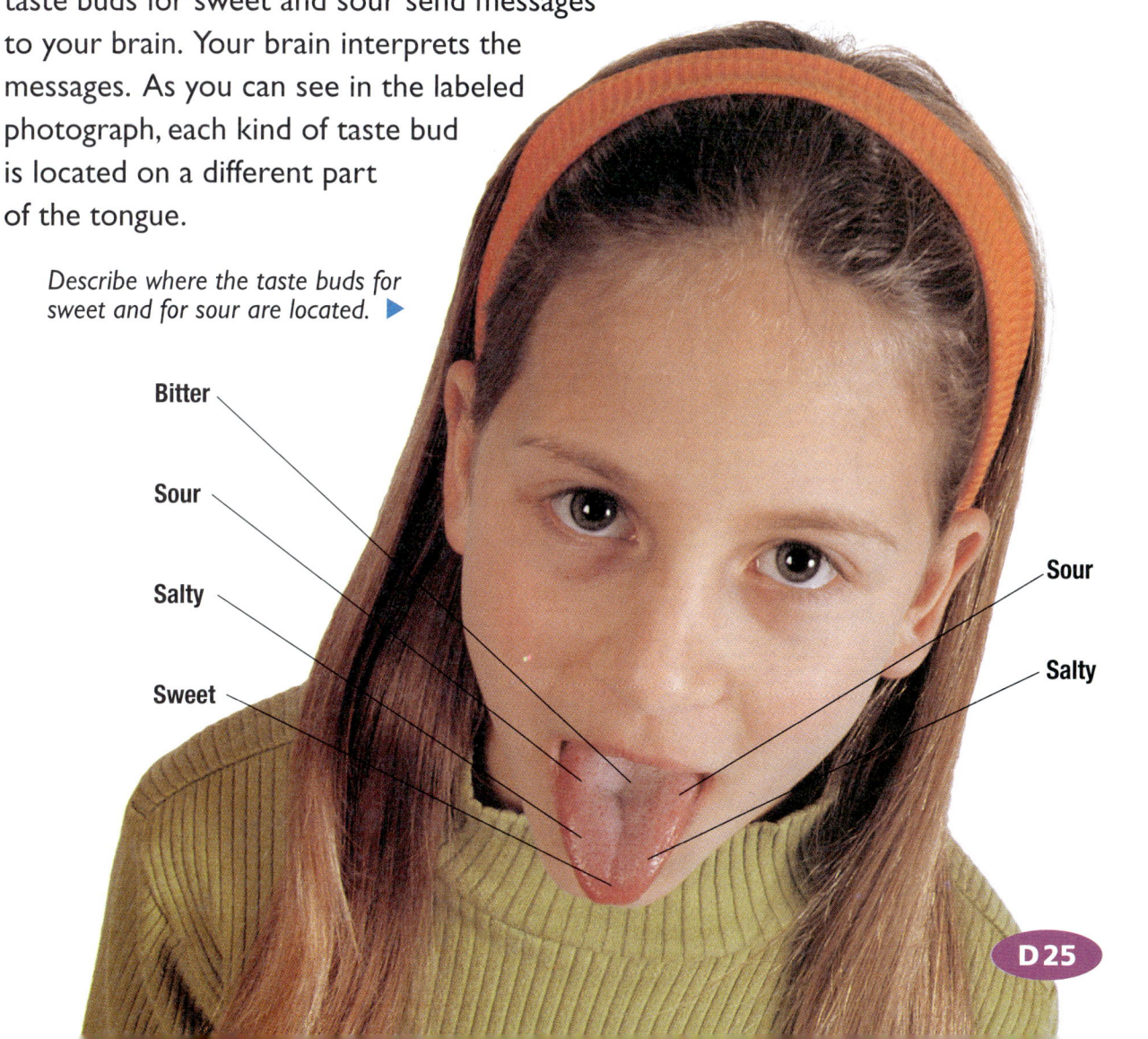

Describe where the taste buds for sweet and for sour are located. ▶

Bitter

Sour

Salty

Sweet

Sour

Salty

D 25

Nerve to brain
Nerve cells
Air space

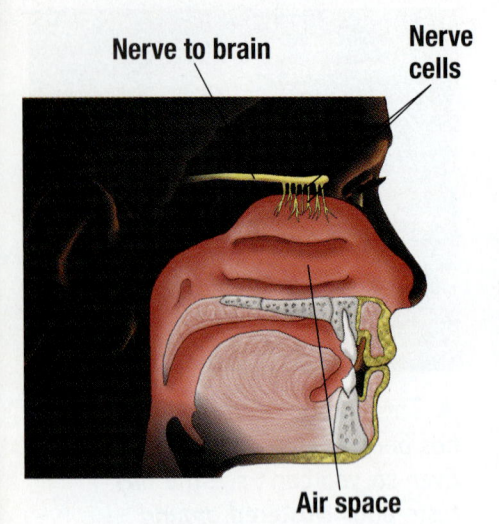

▲ As you breathe in air, smells also enter the nose.

As you might guess, the nerve cells for your sense of smell are in your nose. When you breathe in through your nose, the air moves into a space. You can see in the drawing that nerve cells line the top of this space. Each nerve cell has nerve endings that are like tiny hairs. When a smell enters your nose, these nerve endings gather information about the smell. They send a message to your brain. Your brain tells you what you smell. Look at the picture. What do you suppose the girl's brain is telling her?

When it comes to eating, your nose and tongue work together. As you eat, both sense organs send information to your brain. The brain puts this information together and tells you the flavor of the food. When you have a stuffy nose, your brain does not get as much information as usual. Food seems to lack flavor. That's why you may not enjoy eating when you have a cold.

Nerve cells in your nose gather information about all kinds of smells, both bad and good. ▼

Lesson 3 Review

1. What do nerve cells do?
2. What do nerve endings in your skin do?
3. How does the retina help you see?
4. How do your tongue and nose work together?
5. **Graphic Sources**
   Copy the picture of the nose and trace the path of a smell through the nose.

Experiment Activity

Experimenting with the Sense of Smell

Materials

- 6 medicine cups with lids
- masking tape
- marker
- 1 graduated plastic cup
- water
- dropper
- mint extract
- plastic spoon
- large container

Process Skills

- formulating questions and hypotheses
- identifying and controlling variables
- experimenting
- collecting and interpreting data
- communicating

State the Problem

Do smell thresholds vary among students?

Formulate Your Hypothesis

The smell threshold is the lowest concentration of a substance that a person can smell. Do most students have a similar smell threshold or will there be variation? Write your **hypothesis.**

Identify and Control the Variables

The smell threshold of different students is the **variable** you will test. The same testing procedure must be performed for each student. Each student must smell the same concentrations of mint solution and a control that is unscented.

Test Your Hypothesis

Follow these steps to perform an **experiment.**

1 Make a chart like the one on the next page. Use your chart to record your data.

2 Use a marker and masking tape to label the medicine cups from 0 to 5. Fill medicine cup 0 with water. This will be a control, with no scent.

3 Fill a graduated cup with 240 mL of water. Add 2 drops of mint extract (Photo A). Stir with a plastic spoon.

Photo A

Continued →

D27

Experiment Activity

Continued

Photo B

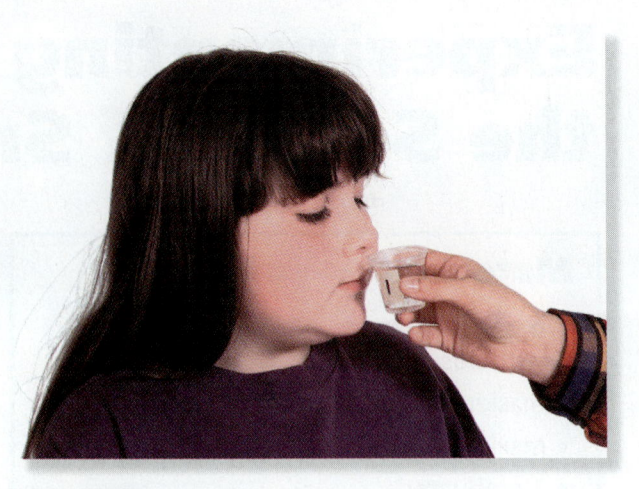

Photo C

④ Open medicine cup 5 and fill it with mint solution. Replace the lid.

⑤ Pour mint solution out of the graduated cup into the large container until there is 120 mL remaining in the cup. Add water to the cup until it is filled to 240 mL. Stir with the plastic spoon. Fill medicine cup 4 with this solution. The mint concentration of cup 4 is now half the concentration of cup 5. Replace the lid.

⑥ Repeat step 5 for medicine cups 3, 2, and 1 (Photo B). Arrange the medicine cups from 0 (no scent) to 5 (highest mint concentration).

⑦ Open medicine cup 0 and have your partner sniff the control. Repeat with increasing concentrations of mint solution, starting with medicine cup 1, until the student can identify the smell as mint (Photo C). **Collect data** by recording the number of the identified concentration in your chart.

⑧ Repeat the test until all of your group members have been tested.

⑨ Obtain the test results from other groups and add them to your chart.

Collect Your Data

Student	Smell threshold concentration
1	
2	
3	
4	

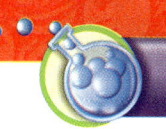

Interpret Your Data

1. Label a piece of grid paper as shown. Use the data from your chart to make a bar graph on your grid paper.

2. Study your graph. Which concentration did most students identify as their smell threshold? Describe how the smell threshold varied, if it did, among students.

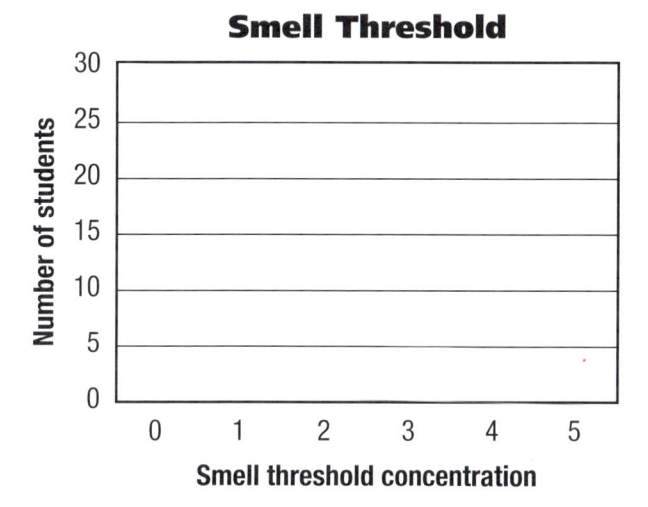

Smell Threshold

Number of students (0, 5, 10, 15, 20, 25, 30)
Smell threshold concentration (0, 1, 2, 3, 4, 5)

State Your Conclusions

How do your results compare with your hypothesis? **Communicate** your results. Write an explanation of how the smell threshold for mint does or does not vary among students.

? Inquire Further

Would the smell threshold results be similar with other scents such as vanilla or lemon? Develop a plan to answer this or other questions you may have.

Self-Assessment

- I made a **hypothesis** about smell thresholds.
- I **identified** and **controlled variables.**
- I followed instructions to conduct an **experiment** to test students' smell thresholds for mint.
- I **collected** and **interpreted** data by making a chart and a graph.
- I **communicated** by writing my conclusion explaining how the smell threshold for mint does or does not vary among students.

D29

Chapter 1 Review

Chapter Main Ideas

Lesson 1
• The digestive system changes food into nutrients that body cells use for energy, for growth and repair, and for working well.
• Food is broken down and chemically changed as it moves from the mouth through the esophagus to the stomach and small intestine.

Lesson 2
• The parts of blood are plasma, red blood cells, white blood cells, and platelets, and each part does a different job.
• The three kinds of blood vessels are arteries, capillaries, and veins, and each does a different job.
• Blood moves through each side of the heart in one direction, from the right atrium to the right ventricle and from the left atrium to the left ventricle.

Lesson 3
• Nerve cells are the basic units of the nervous system, which includes the brain, spinal cord, and nerves.
• Nerve cells in the skin gather information about touch, pressure, heat, cold, and pain and send messages to the brain.
• Nerve cells in the eyes gather information about light and send messages to the brain.
• Nerve cells in the tongue and nose gather information about taste and smell and send messages to the brain.

Reviewing Science Words and Concepts

Write the letter of the word or phrase that best completes each sentence.

a. artery
b. atrium
c. capillary
d. digestion
e. enzyme
f. esophagus
g. nerve cell
h. nerve ending
i. nutrient
j. plasma
k. platelet
l. red blood cell
m. saliva
n. sense organ
o. small intestine
p. spinal cord
q. vein
r. ventricle
s. white blood cell

1. A substance in food that the body uses for energy, for growth and repair, or for working well is a ___.
2. The changing of food into forms that body cells can use is called ___.
3. The liquid in the mouth that helps break down food is ___.
4. A chemical that helps the digestive system change food into nutrients is an ___.

5. The food you eat travels from your mouth to your stomach through the ___.

6. Most digestion of food takes place in the ___.

7. The watery part of blood is ___.

8. A blood cell that carries oxygen is a ___.

9. A blood cell that fights germs is a ___.

10. A tiny part of a cell that helps stop bleeding is a ___.

11. A blood vessel that carries blood away from the heart is an ___.

12. A tiny blood vessel with thin walls is a ___.

13. A blood vessel that carries blood to the heart is a ___.

14. A space in the heart that receives blood from veins is an ___.

15. A space in the heart that pumps blood out of the heart is a ___.

16. A body part, such as the nose, that gathers information about the surroundings is a ___.

17. A cell that gathers and carries information in the body is a ___.

18. A tiny branch of a nerve cell that gathers information is a ___.

19. The bundle of nerves that connects the brain with nerves throughout the body is the ___.

Explaining Science

Draw and label a diagram or write a paragraph to answer these questions.

1. How does food change as it moves through the digestive system?

2. How does the blood move through the heart?

3. How do you know when you are touching something soft?

Using Skills

1. Use what you've learned about **capacity** to answer this question: If your heart pumps 7,500 liters of blood each day, how many milliliters of blood does it pump in a day?

2. For fifteen minutes, **observe** your surroundings with all your sense organs. As you do this, make a list of everything you observe. Then arrange the items in your list according to which sense you used.

Critical Thinking

1. Without looking, you take a bite of food. At first, it tastes salty. After you chew the food, it tastes sweet. What might you **infer** about what the food is?

2. Suppose you eat a bite of apple while holding your nose. **Predict** whether the apple will taste the same as an apple usually does. Explain your reasoning.

Sip, Sip. Yum!

Aren't those little cardboard juice containers great? They can go anywhere—no need for a refrigerator! And every sip of that yummy juice helps keep your body systems healthy.

Chapter 2
Keeping Your Body Systems Healthy

Inquiring about Keeping Your Body Systems Healthy

Lesson 1 How Can You Keep Your Digestive System Healthy?
- What are some problems of the digestive system?
- What are some ways to prevent digestive system problems?

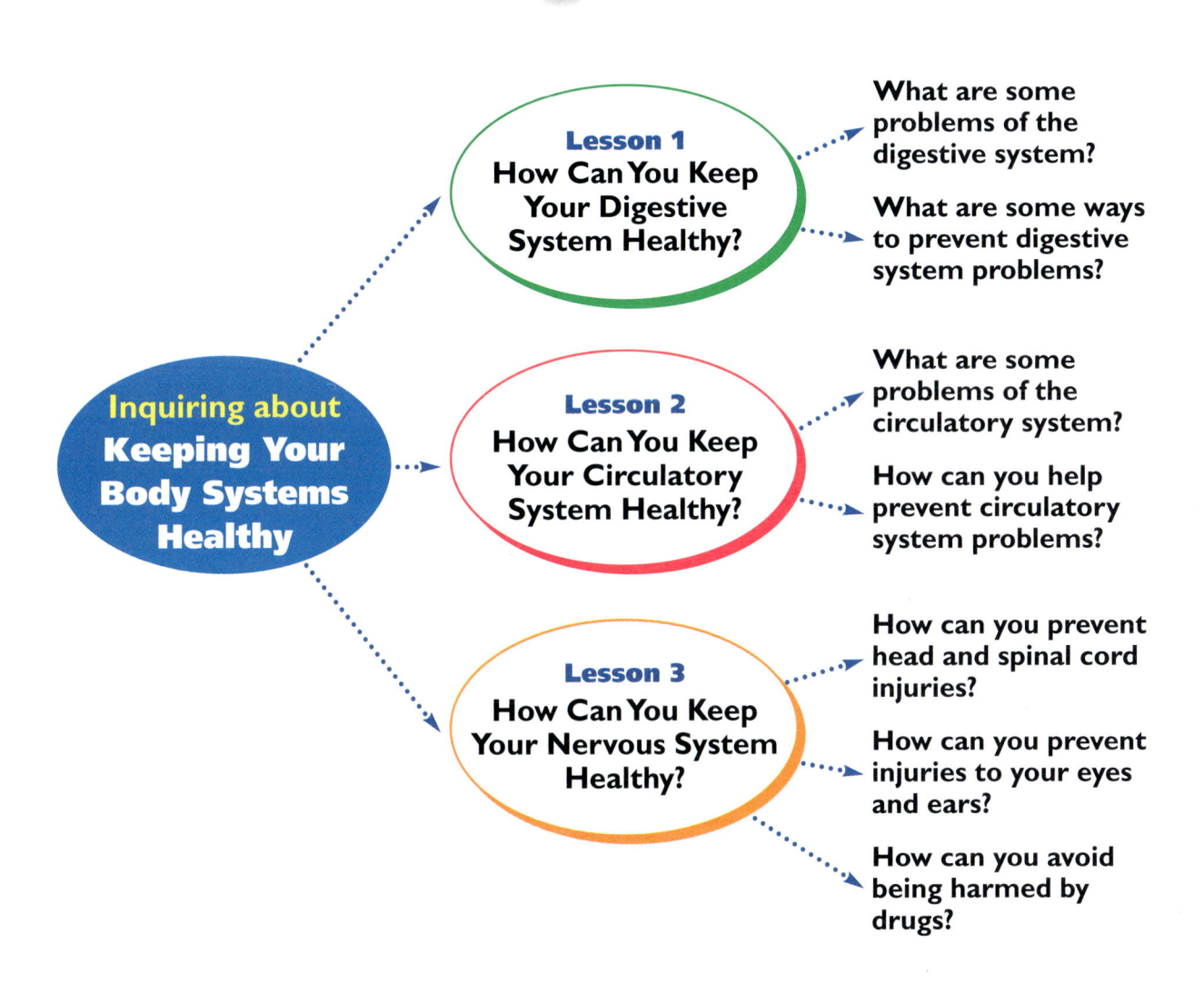

Lesson 2 How Can You Keep Your Circulatory System Healthy?
- What are some problems of the circulatory system?
- How can you help prevent circulatory system problems?

Lesson 3 How Can You Keep Your Nervous System Healthy?
- How can you prevent head and spinal cord injuries?
- How can you prevent injuries to your eyes and ears?
- How can you avoid being harmed by drugs?

Copy the chapter graphic organizer onto your own paper. This organizer shows you what the whole chapter is all about. As you read the lessons and do the activities, look for answers to the questions and write them on your organizer.

Explore Activity

Exploring Food Labels

Process Skills
- collecting and interpreting data
- communicating

Materials
- masking tape
- marker
- 3 empty cereal packages

Explore

1. Use the masking tape and marker to label the cereals A, B, and C.

2. Study the Nutrition Facts section of the cereal A package. **Collect data** by recording the serving size, total fat, and dietary fiber.

3. Repeat step 2 for cereal B and cereal C.

Reflect

1. In this chapter, you will learn why you should eat little fat and lots of fiber for good health. **Interpret** your **data.** Based on fat and fiber content, does one cereal stand out as the most healthful choice? Why or why not?

2. **Communicate.** Discuss your findings with the class.

Inquire Further

Are granola bars a more healthful food choice than the cereals you studied? Develop a plan to answer this or other questions you may have.

Reading for Science

Identifying Cause and Effect

You know that your heart pumps blood through blood vessels in your body. The heart contracting causes the blood to be pushed out of the heart. The blood moving out of the heart through the blood vessels is the effect. As you read this chapter, look for examples of cause and effect.

Example
In Lesson 1, *How Can You Keep Your Digestive System Healthy?*, you will read about the causes and effects of digestive system problems. Make a chart like the one below to help keep track of the causes and effects of these problems. In the last row of your chart, list the ways you can help avoid the problems.

	Indigestion	Diarrhea	Constipation
Causes			
Effects			
Ways to Help			

▼ *Did you know that foods high in fiber are good for your digestive system?*

Talk About It!

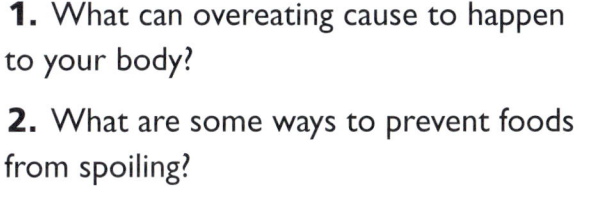

1. What can overeating cause to happen to your body?

2. What are some ways to prevent foods from spoiling?

What's the Big Idea?

Lesson 1

How Can You Keep Your Digestive System Healthy?

You will learn:
- about some problems of the digestive system.
- some ways to prevent digestive system problems.

Birthday parties. Thanksgiving dinner. Family picnics. Saturday at the theme park. All these occasions mean food and fun. Sometimes, though, the fun ends with "UUHH! Why did I eat so much?"

Glossary

indigestion (in/də jes/chən), one or more symptoms, such as stomachache, that occur when the body has difficulty digesting food

Digestive System Problems

If you've ever eaten too much, as the girl in the picture has, you may have gotten a stomachache. Stomachaches are one form of indigestion. Indigestion is not a disease. Instead, **indigestion** includes various symptoms that you may feel when your digestive system has trouble doing its job. For example, you may have a burning feeling in your esophagus, or you may feel as if you are about to vomit, or "throw up."

◀ Sometimes eating too much can give you a stomachache.

In addition to overeating, causes of indigestion can include eating too fast and neglecting to chew food thoroughly. Eating foods and spices, such as those in the picture, can also cause indigestion. Another cause of indigestion might be eating when you are angry or otherwise upset.

Diarrhea is another problem that you may have had. Diarrhea occurs when the solid waste leaving the large intestine has too much water in it. Like stomachache, diarrhea is a symptom, not a disease. Emotional upset is one possible cause of diarrhea. Certain germs that get into the digestive system are another possible cause.

Sometimes, diarrhea is a symptom of food poisoning. A few foods, such as certain wild mushrooms, are naturally poisonous. Other foods can become poisonous when germs get in the food and spoil it. Freezing and canning are two methods that food companies use to try to keep foods from spoiling. However, germs can get in foods that are stored improperly.

Constipation is a different kind of digestive problem. It occurs when solid waste becomes dry and hard and difficult to eliminate from the body. Causes of constipation include not drinking enough water and not eating enough fiber. You will read more about fiber and water on pages D38 and D39.

Hot peppers and spices may taste good, but they can cause indigestion. ▼

Ways to Prevent Digestive Problems

You can prevent many digestive problems. For example, to help prevent indigestion, try not to overeat. Also, eat slowly and chew your food well. If spicy foods give you indigestion, avoid them. If you are very angry or otherwise upset, try to calm down before eating.

Food poisoning also can be prevented. Germs grow best in warm, moist places. Store foods such as meat, milk, cheese, eggs, fresh vegetables, and leftovers in the refrigerator to keep them cold. If any food looks or smells different than usual, do not taste it to decide whether it is spoiled. Tell an adult so that he or she can throw it away. To keep germs out of your digestive system, wash your hands with soap and water before you prepare or eat food. You should also wash fresh fruits and vegetables. Always use clean knives, forks, spoons, and dishes too. The pictures on these two pages show three more ways to help your digestive system work its best.

Foods that are low in fat and high in fiber are good for your digestive system. ▼

First, eat a healthful diet. Limit the amount of fried foods and other fatty foods that you eat. Instead, eat plenty of fruits, vegetables, and whole-grain breads and cereals. Those foods contain the material called fiber. Fiber helps food move through your digestive system properly. It helps prevent both constipation and diarrhea.

Second, drink plenty of water. Your entire body, including your digestive system, needs water to be healthy. In particular, water helps prevent constipation. Eating fruit, drinking fruit juices, and drinking low-fat or nonfat milk are other good ways to get water into your body.

Third, exercise regularly. Exercise helps keep your digestive system in good working order and helps prevent constipation. However, wait at least an hour after you eat before doing vigorous exercise. This will help prevent the painful tightening of the muscles known as cramps.

▲ Vigorous exercise is good for you, but not right after eating! During digestion, a lot of blood flows to the digestive organs. This means that less blood is available for other body parts, including muscles. Cramps may result. Mild activity, such as you might do during recess, shouldn't cause any problems after a meal.

You need to replace the water that your body uses and loses each day. Drink extra water when the weather is hot or when you are working or playing hard. ▶

Lesson 1 Review

1. List three possible causes of indigestion.
2. Why is it important to eat plenty of fruits, vegetables, and whole-grain breads and cereals?
3. **Main Idea**
   What is the main idea of the first paragraph on this page?

D 39

What's the Big Idea?

You will learn:
- about some problems of the circulatory system.
- how you can help prevent circulatory system problems.

Glossary

anemia (ə nē′mē ə), a condition in which the number of healthy red blood cells or the amount of hemoglobin is low

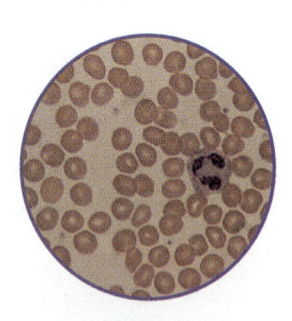

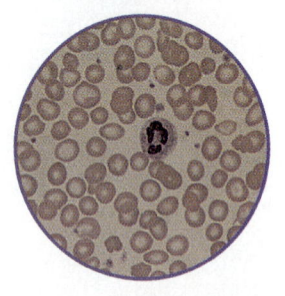

▲ Here you see healthy red blood cells (top) and the red blood cells of a person with one kind of anemia (bottom).

Lesson 2

How Can You Keep Your Circulatory System Healthy?

Only older people need to take care of their circulatory systems, right? Not really! Some circulatory problems can begin in childhood. The good news is that there's a lot you can do to prevent such problems.

Circulatory System Problems

Some circulatory problems affect the heart or the blood vessels. Other problems affect the blood. **Anemia** is a condition in which the number of healthy red blood cells is low or the amount of iron in the red blood cells is low. There are many different forms and causes of anemia.

The most common form of anemia occurs when a person's diet does not provide enough iron. The body needs this mineral to produce hemoglobin, the substance in red blood cells that carries oxygen. Too little iron means that the blood does not carry enough oxygen to body cells. Someone with this form of anemia may feel tired all the time and be very pale. The pictures show the difference between healthy red blood cells and red blood cells that do not have enough iron.

Lack of certain vitamins or exposure to dangerous chemicals also can cause anemia. Some kinds of anemia are inherited—that is, they are passed from parents to children.

High blood pressure is another problem of the circulatory system. In this disease, blood is pumped through the arteries with more force than is needed to move the blood through the body. Over a period of years, high blood pressure can damage the heart, brain, other organs, and blood vessels.

Most people with high blood pressure have no symptoms of the disease. A doctor or nurse usually finds the problem. Children rarely have high blood pressure. Still, it's a good idea to have your blood pressure measured as part of your regular health checkup, as the girl in the picture does.

In most cases of high blood pressure, doctors cannot tell the exact cause. People may inherit a tendency to have high blood pressure. In these people, being overweight, smoking, or eating too much salt may cause the disease to develop.

Glossary

high blood pressure (presh′ər), a disease in which blood is pumped through the arteries with too much force

Blood pressure is the force of the blood on the walls of arteries as it is pumped through the arteries. Blood pressure is measured in the main artery of the arm. ▼

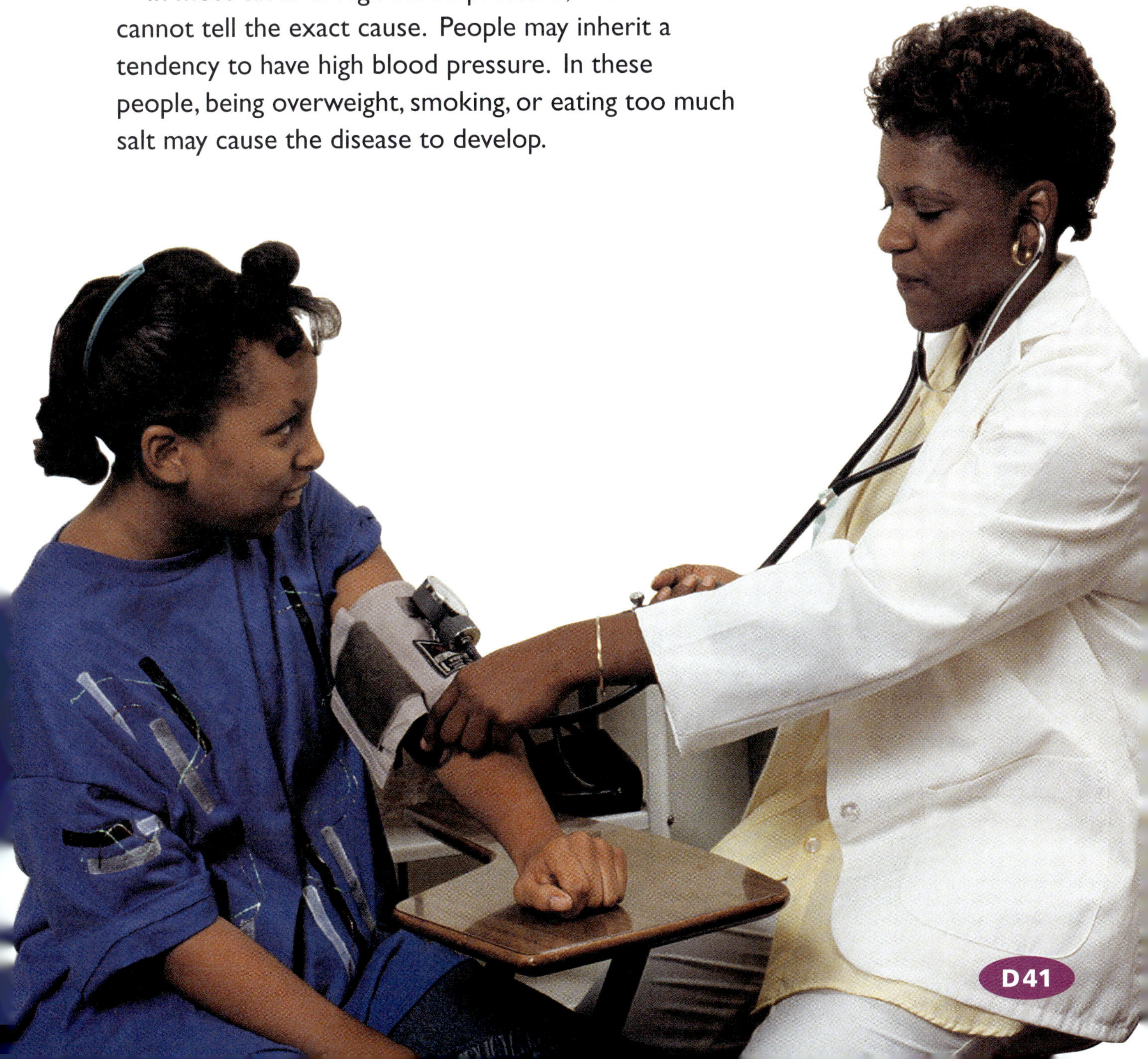

Glossary

atherosclerosis (ath′ər ō sklə rō′sis), a disease in which fatty substances build up on the inside walls of arteries

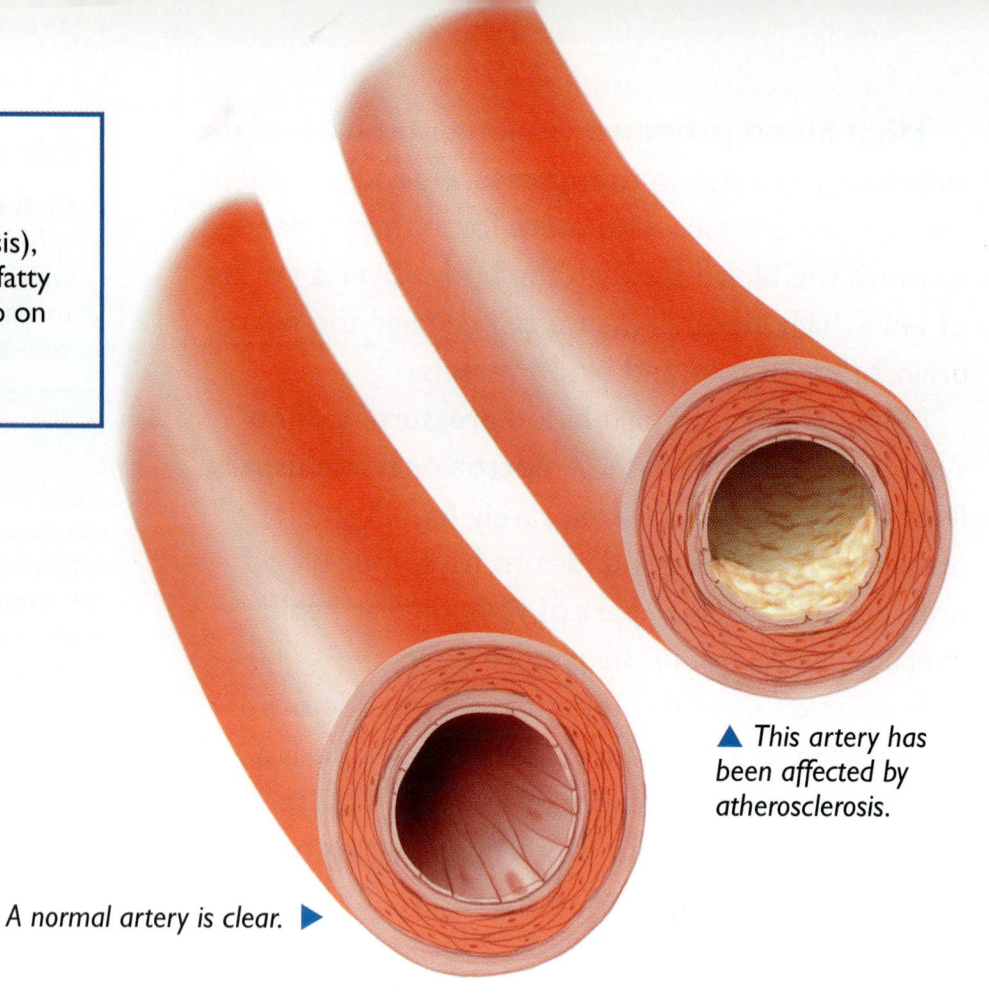

▲ This artery has been affected by atherosclerosis.

A normal artery is clear. ▶

A circulatory problem called **atherosclerosis** occurs when fatty substances in the blood stick to the inside walls of arteries. Some of the fatty substances come from digested food. Over a period of years, the arteries become partly or completely blocked. The pictures above show a normal artery and one that is partly blocked by fatty substances.

As atherosclerosis develops, the flow of blood through the arteries decreases. As a result, some body cells may not get enough oxygen. If an artery carrying blood to the heart muscle becomes blocked, some cells in the heart muscle may die from lack of oxygen. This event is called a heart attack. If an artery carrying blood to the brain becomes blocked, some cells in the brain may die from lack of oxygen. This event is called a stroke. Some people recover from a heart attack or stroke. However, either event can cause lasting damage and even death.

Ways to Prevent Circulatory System Problems

Anemia can affect people of all ages. Children usually do not have heart attacks or strokes, but children as young as age three have been found to have early signs of atherosclerosis. High blood pressure in adults may be triggered by habits that begin in childhood. It makes sense to do all you can to keep your circulatory system healthy—starting right now!

Your diet is a good place to begin. You can help prevent the most common form of anemia by eating foods rich in iron. Such foods include meat, poultry, fish, eggs, and dry beans. What iron-rich foods do you see in the picture?

Fat is a nutrient that you need for energy. However, you don't need a lot of it. You know that fatty substances can clog arteries. Too much fat in the diet also can make a person overweight, which puts a strain on the circulatory system. To reduce the fat in your diet, limit the amount of fried foods and high-fat foods from animals, such as meat and eggs. Choose low-fat or nonfat milk, cheese, and yogurt over other dairy products.

Fruits, vegetables, and grain products should make up most of your diet. You need only two or three daily servings of foods like meat, poultry, fish, and eggs. You also need only two or three daily servings of dairy products such as milk. ▼

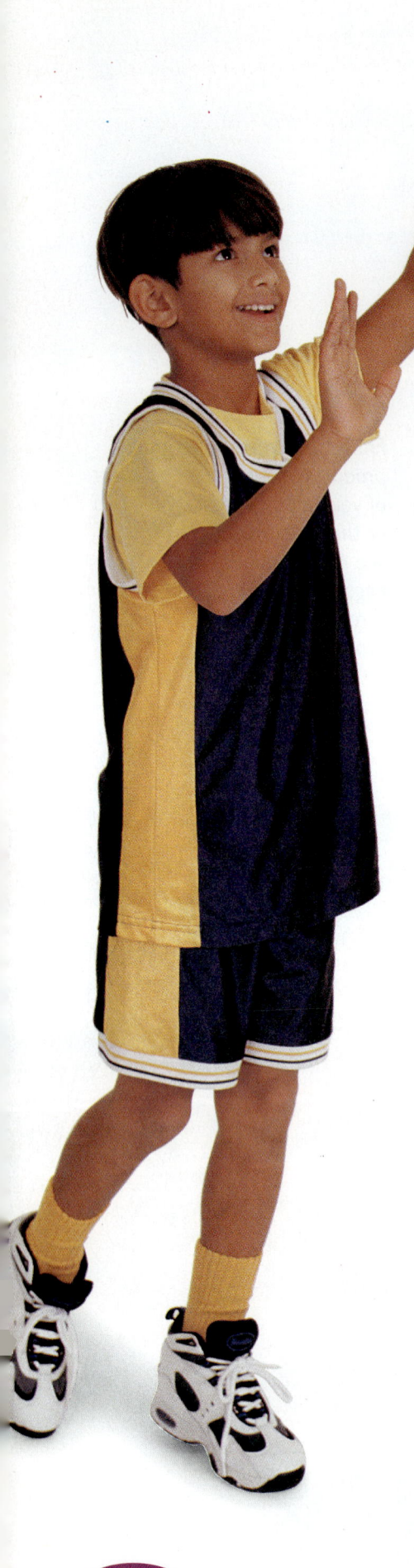

◀ *This boy is doing a lot more than improving his basketball shot. He's helping his heart too! Playing active games such as basketball is a good way to exercise. Other good ways include bicycling, running, swimming, jumping rope, and cross-country skiing.*

You've read that too much salt may lead to high blood pressure in some people. Your body needs the sodium found in salt. However, a healthy diet contains all the sodium you need. It's a good idea to limit the amount of salt you add to food. Also, choose packaged foods whose labels show salt or sodium low on the list of ingredients.

Another way to help your circulatory system is to get plenty of exercise, as the child in the picture does. Regular, vigorous exercise strengthens the muscles, including the heart muscle. A strong heart can pump more blood with each beat and rest longer between beats. Also, exercise causes extra blood vessels to grow in the heart. This increases the blood supply to the heart.

Exercise has other benefits. Exercise helps maintain a normal body weight. It helps keep blood pressure low. It also helps keep fatty substances from building up inside arteries. Therefore, exercise may lower the risk of heart attacks and strokes.

A drug is a substance that causes changes in the way the body works. You can help keep your circulatory system healthy by avoiding drugs that harm it. One such drug is nicotine, which is found in cigarettes and other products made from tobacco. Nicotine strains the heart by making it beat too fast. Nicotine also narrows the blood vessels, which raises blood pressure and decreases the flow of blood through the body.

Smoke from cigarettes and other tobacco products contains carbon monoxide, a poisonous gas. Carbon monoxide replaces some oxygen in the blood. This means that a smoker's body cells do not get all the oxygen they need. Smoking also contributes to atherosclerosis. Smokers are more likely to have heart attacks and strokes than nonsmokers are.

Marijuana and cocaine also can harm the circulatory system. Both drugs make the heart beat too fast. Cocaine also narrows blood vessels and raises blood pressure. It can cause a dangerously irregular heartbeat or heart attack.

Tobacco products, marijuana, and cocaine are not good for your circulatory system or any other part of your body. Don't use them!

The red blood cells of people who smoke don't carry as much oxygen as the red blood cells of people who don't smoke. ▶

Lesson 2 Review

1. What harm can be done by fatty substances in the blood?
2. What are three ways that exercise helps the circulatory system?
3. **Cause and Effect**
   What are some effects that can be caused by using marijuana and cocaine?

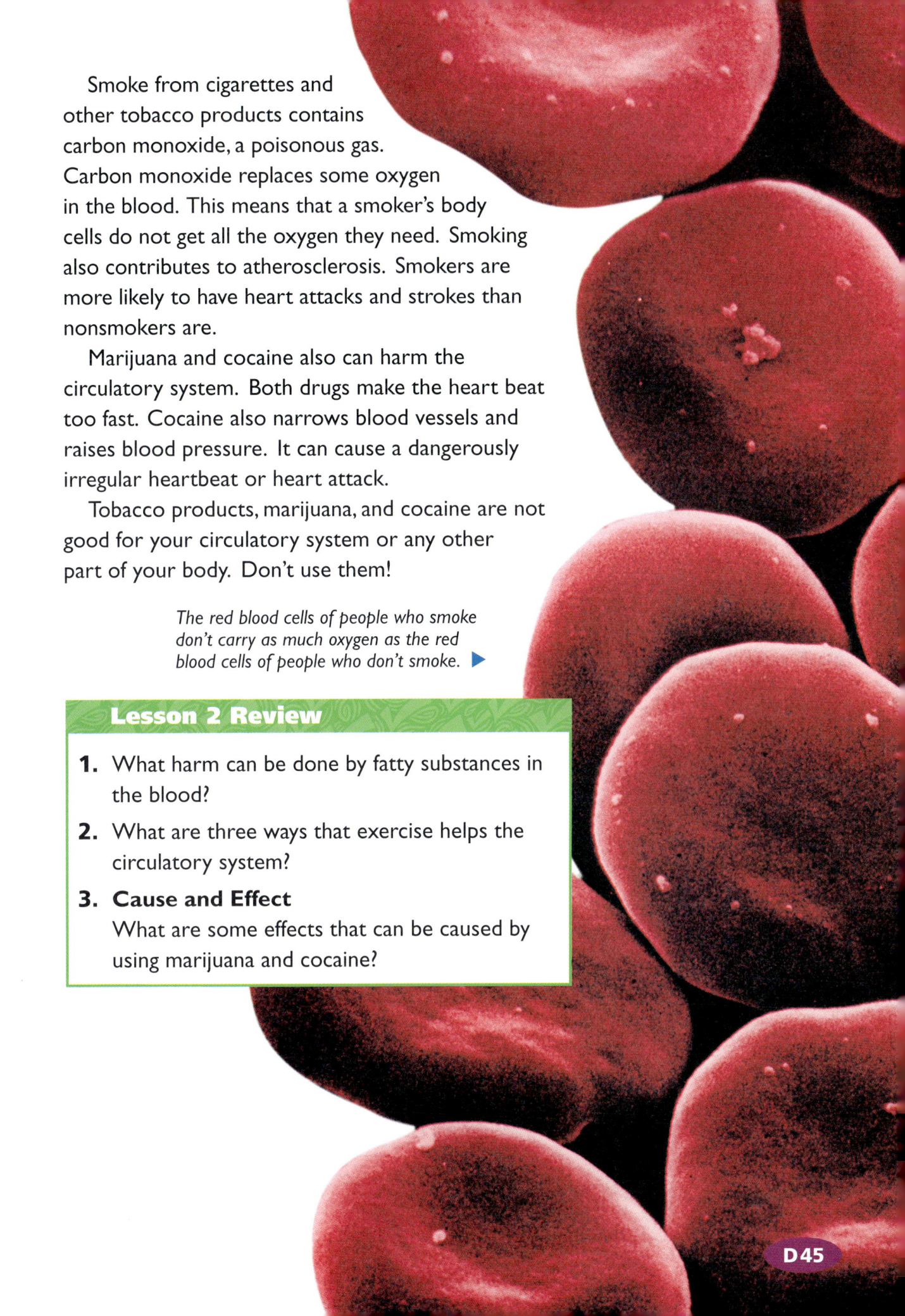

Investigate Activity

Investigating How the Heart Works

Process Skills
- estimating and measuring
- observing
- inferring
- communicating

Materials
- clock with a second hand
- ball

Getting Ready
By trying to make your hand and arm muscles work at the same rate as your heart, you can appreciate how hard your heart works. You also can gain understanding of the importance of exercise.

Follow This Procedure

1 Make a chart like the one shown. Use your chart to record your measurements and observations.

Resting heart rate	
Length of time I was able to squeeze the ball	
Observations	

2 Place your arm on a desk, palm up. Place the first two fingers of your other hand against your upturned wrist near the base of your thumb (Photo A). Press gently until you can feel your pulse.

3 Watching the clock, count your pulse for ten seconds. Stop counting, write the number down, and multiply it by six. This **measurement** is your resting heart rate.

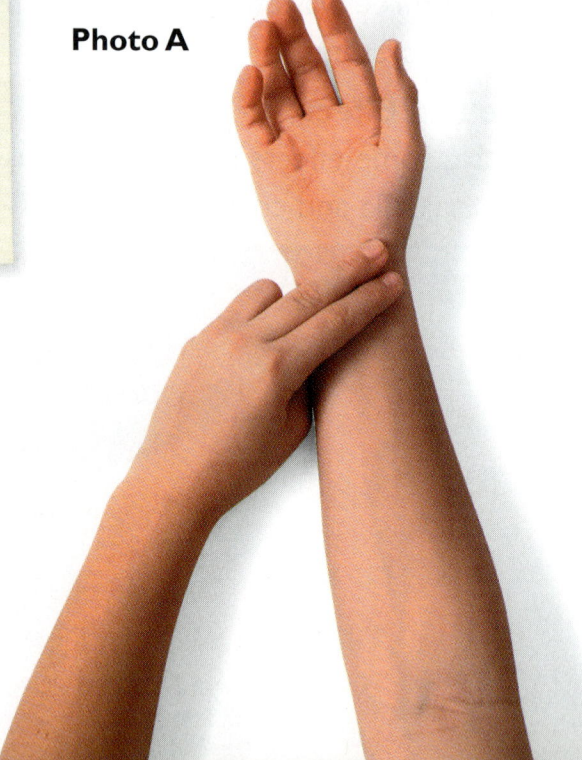

Photo A

Photo B

4 Now hold the ball in one hand. Use your right hand if you are right-handed or your left hand if you are left-handed. Squeeze the ball hard (Photo B) and then relax your grip. This is about the amount of force your heart puts forth with each beat.

5 Again, watching the clock, try to squeeze the ball at the same rate as your heart rate. For example, if your heart rate is 80 beats per minute, squeeze the ball 80 times per minute. How long can you go without slowing? without stopping? Record your time. How do the muscles of your hand and arm feel when you do stop? Record your **observations.**

Self-Monitoring
Have I correctly completed all the steps?

Interpret Your Results

1. Make an **inference.** How is your heart muscle different from the muscles in your hands and arms?

2. A strong heart can pump more blood with each beat and rest longer between beats. Make an inference. If you began a regular exercise program today and continued for a month, how might your resting heart rate change?

3. **Communicate.** Imagine that your heart can talk. Write what it might say to persuade you to lower your resting heart rate.

Inquire Further

Besides exercise, what other things affect a person's resting heart rate? Develop a plan to answer this or other questions you may have.

Self-Assessment

- I followed instructions to **measure** my resting heart rate.
- I followed instructions to try to make my hand and arm muscles work at the same rate as my heart rate.
- I recorded my **observations.**
- I made **inferences** about how my heart differs from other muscles and how regular exercise might affect my resting heart rate.
- I **communicated** by writing what my heart might say to encourage me to lower my resting heart rate.

What's the Big Idea?

You will learn:
- how to prevent head and spinal cord injuries.
- how to prevent injuries to your eyes and ears.
- how to avoid being harmed by drugs.

Lesson 3

How Can You Keep Your Nervous System Healthy?

The scene you see here couldn't have happened when your parents were your age. In-line skates hadn't been invented! Few, if any, skaters wore pads or helmets. **OOPS!** When they fell down, it could really hurt.

Preventing Head and Spinal Cord Injuries

Some people still don't understand why they need to wear a helmet for activities such as in-line skating. They believe their skull will protect them if they fall and hit their head. It's true that the bones of the skull do a good job of protecting the brain most of the time. However, a hard blow to an unprotected head still can cause harm. The skull may crack. Even if it doesn't, the blow may cause a sudden movement of the brain inside the skull. The brain may even be bruised.

◀ Getting injured is no fun at all. That's why this boy protects his knees, elbows, wrists, and head when he goes in-line skating.

A condition known as a **concussion** is one possible result of a sudden movement of the brain. In most cases of concussion, the person loses consciousness for a short time. Other possible symptoms include memory loss, headache, and blurred vision. The symptoms go away after a while.

More serious head injuries can cause lasting damage to the brain. Also, injuries to the spine can cause lasting damage to the spinal cord. The body cannot make new nerve cells to replace nerve cells that have been damaged or have died. Some head and spine injuries are so severe that they cause death.

Wear a helmet, such as the ones shown, when you do any activity in which you could be struck on the head or could fall and hit your head. Such activities include in-line skating, skateboarding, and bicycling. College and professional football and hockey players wear helmets, as do baseball and softball players when they go to bat. If you play those sports, you should wear a helmet too.

Do you like to swim and dive? If so, be sure to find out how deep the water is before you dive in. Do this whether you are at a pool or a natural body of water such as a lake. If you dive into water that is too shallow, you could hit the bottom. You could suffer a head or spine injury as a result. Also, if you are diving off a board or platform, be sure to jump in such a way that you do not hit your head, neck, or back on it.

> **Glossary**
>
> **concussion**
> (kən kush′ən), a condition caused by a sudden movement of the brain inside the skull, usually involving a brief loss of consciousness

Helmets can protect the brain from damage. ▼

Car accidents are a leading cause of injuries, including head and spine injuries. To be safe in a car, do as the girl at the left does. Always wear your safety belt. Wear it even if you are riding for only a short distance. If possible, sit in the back seat. You're less likely to be injured in the back seat if an accident does occur.

You can prevent head and spine injuries by making safety a part of your daily life. Like the children below, cross streets only at corners and crosswalks. When bicycling, ride on the right-hand side of the street and be sure to obey all traffic signs and signals.

▲ *Buckle up your safety belt every time you ride in a car.*

Cross the street only when no traffic is coming. Look in all directions to be sure. If the corner has a traffic signal, wait for the walk sign or the green light to come on, check to be sure no traffic is coming, and then cross. ▼

D 50

Preventing Injuries to Eyes and Ears

The bones around your eyes help protect the eyes from blows. Your ability to blink and your eyelashes also help protect your eyes by keeping dust and other things out. Tears wash away some things that do get in the eyes.

You can do your part to protect your sense of sight. Chemicals, wood chips, and other things can harm your eyes. Like the students at the right, wear safety goggles when you do an experiment or other activity that might send something splashing or flying into your eyes.

Never throw sand, dirt, balls, or other objects toward anyone's eyes. Don't wave sharp objects around either. If you get something in your eyes, don't rub them. Get an adult's help right away.

Bright sunlight can also damage your eyes, so never look directly at the sun. Be sure to wear sunglasses with UV protection outdoors on sunny days. What else is the girl at the right doing to protect her eyes from the sun?

▲ Don't take chances with your eyesight. Wear safety goggles when you do science experiments, when you work with tools, and when you use chemicals, such as cleansers, at home.

She's cool—and smart! She knows that good-quality sunglasses and a hat with a brim protect her eyes from the sun's damaging rays. ▶

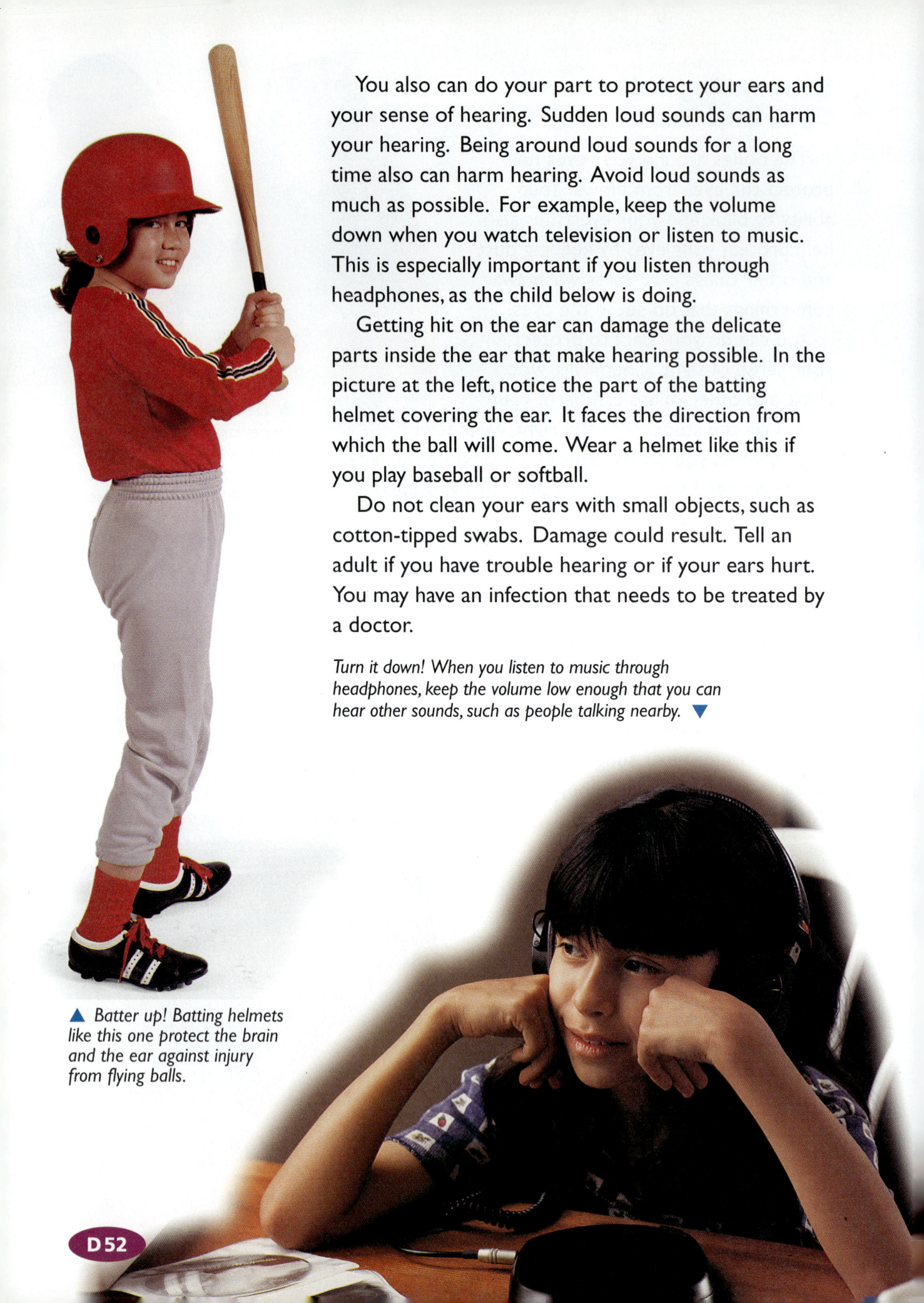

You also can do your part to protect your ears and your sense of hearing. Sudden loud sounds can harm your hearing. Being around loud sounds for a long time also can harm hearing. Avoid loud sounds as much as possible. For example, keep the volume down when you watch television or listen to music. This is especially important if you listen through headphones, as the child below is doing.

Getting hit on the ear can damage the delicate parts inside the ear that make hearing possible. In the picture at the left, notice the part of the batting helmet covering the ear. It faces the direction from which the ball will come. Wear a helmet like this if you play baseball or softball.

Do not clean your ears with small objects, such as cotton-tipped swabs. Damage could result. Tell an adult if you have trouble hearing or if your ears hurt. You may have an infection that needs to be treated by a doctor.

Turn it down! When you listen to music through headphones, keep the volume low enough that you can hear other sounds, such as people talking nearby. ▼

▲ *Batter up! Batting helmets like this one protect the brain and the ear against injury from flying balls.*

Saying No to Drugs

Many drugs can affect the brain. They can change the way a person thinks, feels, or acts. To keep your brain—and your whole body—healthy, you need to make wise decisions about drugs. For most drugs, your decision should be the same as the decision made by the girl in the picture: No!

Medicines are one kind of drug that can be helpful to health. Different medicines treat, cure, or prevent various health problems. An over-the-counter medicine is a medicine that people can buy without a doctor's order. People use such medicines for health problems that are not serious, such as a mild headache. A prescription medicine is a medicine that can be bought only with a doctor's order. A pharmacist carries out the order and gets the medicine ready.

Medicines are safe only when used correctly. You should take medicine only with the help of a doctor, a nurse, or an adult who is responsible for you. The adult should read and carefully follow all the directions on the medicine's label. The adult also should make sure that no one else takes a prescription medicine meant for you. The medicine could harm someone else.

The buttons on this girl's backpack make it clear how she feels about harmful drugs. ▼

D53

Alcohol is a drug found in beer, wine, and liquor. Alcohol slows down the work of the brain. This in turn slows down other parts of the body. Someone who drinks alcohol may be unable to think, speak, or see clearly. He or she may walk unsteadily and feel dizzy or sleepy. If a drinker tries to drive a car or a bicycle, an accident may result. Over time, large amounts of alcohol can damage the brain, heart, and digestive organs.

It is against the law to sell alcohol to young people. Certain other drugs, such as marijuana and cocaine, are illegal for people of any age to sell, buy, or use. Marijuana and cocaine harm various parts of the body, including the brain. For example, marijuana users may have trouble learning because they cannot concentrate or remember facts.

You may wonder why people use drugs such as alcohol, marijuana, and cocaine. Some people start using drugs because they are bored. They may try a drug because their friends use it, and they want to feel part of the group. After a while, they may become dependent on a drug. They may believe they cannot get along without it.

Playing team sports such as soccer is just one way to be part of a group without using drugs. What other ways can you think of? ▼

◀ These children have made a choice to be drug-free.

One of the best decisions you can make in life is to say no to drugs such as alcohol, marijuana, and cocaine. That is what the children above have done. They know that there are many healthful ways to have fun and be part of a group. They don't use drugs to try to "belong."

Sometimes saying no is hard. You may fear that others will make fun of you or that you will lose your friends. Talking things over with your family can help you stand firm in your decision to refuse drugs. Also, your school or another organization in your community may offer a program to help you.

Lesson 3 Review

1. Why should you wear a helmet for activities such as in-line skating and bicycling?
2. List two ways to protect your eyes and two ways to protect your ears.
3. Why should you say no to alcohol?
4. **Main Idea**
   What is the main idea of the first paragraph on this page?

Investigate Activity

Conducting a Safety Survey

Process Skills
- collecting and interpreting data
- inferring
- communicating

Materials
- grid paper
- pencil

Getting Ready
In this activity you will conduct a survey to find out how often fourth graders wear helmets when bicycling.

Follow This Procedure

1 Make a chart like the one shown. Use your chart to record your data.

Use of bicycle helmets	Tally of students	Totals
Always		
Usually		
Sometimes		
Never		

2 Decide how many students to survey about their use of bicycle helmets. You might survey your entire class or more than one fourth-grade class. The more students you survey, the more reliable your data will be.

3 Decide how to word your survey question. Here is one possibility: "How often do you wear a helmet when bicycling: always, usually, sometimes, or never?" Write the question at the top of your survey form.

4 Ask each student in your survey group the question that you have written. **Collect data** by making a tally mark for each student's answer in the correct place on the survey form. Then calculate the total number of students that chose each answer.

D 56

Self-Monitoring
Have I correctly completed all the steps?

Interpret Your Results

1. Label a piece of grid paper as shown. If your survey group is larger than 50, add numbers as needed. Use the data from your survey form to make a bar graph on the grid paper.

2. Study your graph. **Interpret data** by writing a paragraph that summarizes what the graph shows about the helmet-wearing practices of fourth graders.

Bicycle Helmet Use by Fourth Graders

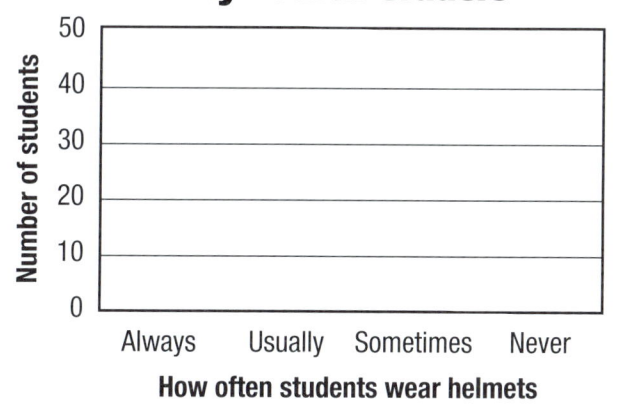

Number of students: 0, 10, 20, 30, 40, 50
How often students wear helmets: Always, Usually, Sometimes, Never

3. Make an **inference.** What attitudes toward bicycle safety and helmets do fourth graders have? **Communicate.** Discuss your inference with classmates.

Inquire Further

How might the results of the survey be different after students see a presentation on bicycle safety, or participate in other bicycle safety activities? Develop a plan to answer this or other questions you may have.

Self-Assessment

- I followed instructions to conduct a survey about use of bicycle helmets.
- I **recorded** my **data** in a survey form and **interpreted** my **data** by making and studying a bar graph.
- I wrote a paragraph to summarize the data in the bar graph.
- I made an **inference** about the safety attitudes of fourth graders.
- I **communicated** by discussing my inference with the class.

D 57

Chapter 2 Review

Chapter Main Ideas

Lesson 1
• Problems of the digestive system can include indigestion, diarrhea, and constipation.
• Ways to prevent digestive system problems include not overeating, keeping germs out of food, eating foods low in fat and high in fiber, drinking plenty of water, and exercising regularly.

Lesson 2
• Problems of the circulatory system can include anemia, high blood pressure, and atherosclerosis.
• Ways to prevent circulatory system problems include eating foods rich in iron, limiting fat and salt in the diet, getting plenty of vigorous exercise, and avoiding harmful drugs such as nicotine.

Lesson 3
• Ways to prevent head injuries include wearing a helmet for activities such as bicycling, being careful when diving into water, and wearing a safety belt when riding in a car.
• Ways to prevent injuries to the eyes and ears include wearing sunglasses outdoors, wearing safety goggles for certain activities, avoiding loud sounds, and protecting the ears from flying objects.

• Ways to avoid being harmed by drugs include using medicines correctly and saying no to drugs such as alcohol, marijuana, and cocaine.

Reviewing Science Words and Concepts

Write the letter of the word or phrase that best completes each sentence.

a. anemia
b. atherosclerosis
c. concussion
d. high blood pressure
e. indigestion

1. A symptom that occurs when the body has difficulty digesting food is known as ___.
2. A condition in which there is a low number of healthy red blood cells or a low amount of iron in the blood cells is ___.
3. A disease in which blood is pumped through the arteries with too much force is ___.
4. A buildup of fatty substances on the inside walls of arteries is known as ___.
5. A hard blow to the head can cause a ___.

Explaining Science

Draw and label a diagram or write a sentence or paragraph to answer these questions.

1. What are four things you can do to help your digestive system?

2. What are three steps you can take to keep your circulatory system healthy?

3. How can you protect your brain from the time you leave school today until you go to bed?

Using Skills

1. Use **cause** and **effect** to explain how the use of drugs can harm your circulatory system.

2. **Collect data** about ways to keep the digestive system and the circulatory system healthy. Make a Venn diagram. Label the left-hand circle *Ways to Help the Digestive System*. Label the right-hand circle *Ways to Help the Circulatory System*. Fill in the three sections of the diagram. **Interpret** the **data** to find out what ways help both the digestive system and the circulatory system.

3. One of your friends is tired all the time. She does not have the energy to play games like your other friends do. What might you **infer** about the condition of your friend's blood?

Critical Thinking

1. Your friend spends most of his free time watching TV and playing computer games. If he continues to do this, what might you **infer** about the health of his circulatory system as he grows up?

2. One Friday after school, a group of older children invite you to go to the park. They hint that someone will be there with cigarettes and beer for them. **Make a decision** about what you should do. Why?

3. When you arrive home after school one afternoon, you make an unpleasant discovery: You accidentally left a carton of milk out on the counter that morning. It's been sitting there all day. **Draw a conclusion.** What should you do? What should you not do?

Unit D Review

Reviewing Words and Concepts

Choose at least three words from the Chapter 1 list below. Use the words to write a paragraph that shows how the words are related. Do the same for Chapter 2.

Chapter 1
artery
capillary
plasma
red blood cell
vein
white blood cell

Chapter 2
anemia
atherosclerosis
concussion
high blood
 pressure
indigestion

Reviewing Main Ideas

Each of the statements below is false. Change the underlined word or words to make each statement true.

1. A liquid called <u>nutrient</u> begins the process of digesting food.
2. Chewed food travels through the <u>enzyme</u> on its way from the mouth to the stomach.
3. Each <u>ventricle</u> in the heart receives blood from veins.
4. Nerve cells in your sense organs have tiny branches called <u>spinal cords</u>, which gather information.
5. Two sense organs—your tongue and your <u>skin</u>—work together to help you taste food.
6. Fruits and vegetables contain a material called <u>fat</u>, which helps food move through the digestive system properly.
7. By keeping the <u>intestines</u> clear of fatty substances, exercise may lower the risk of strokes.
8. Cigarettes contain <u>iron</u>, a drug that makes the heart beat fast and narrows the blood vessels.
9. To help prevent head injuries, wear a <u>hat</u> when in-line skating, skateboarding, or bicycling.
10. The sense of <u>sight</u> can be harmed by loud sounds.

Interpreting Data

Use the information on the food label below to answer the questions below. The label shows the amount of nutrients in one serving.

Total Fat	0 g
Saturated Fat	0 g
Cholesterol	0 mg
Sodium	340 mg
Total Carbohydrates	20 g
Dietary Fiber	6 g
Sugars	2 g
Protein	8 g

1. How many grams of fat does one serving of the food contain?

2. Which does the food contain more of, fiber or sugar?

3. In what ways is this food a good choice for your circulatory system? your digestive system?

Communicating Science

1. Draw and label a diagram that shows the order in which these body parts are used during digestion: esophagus, large intestine, mouth, small intestine, stomach. Add a paragraph that summarizes the steps in digestion.

2. Write a paragraph to explain how your sense organs are like one another and different from one another.

3. Write a summary of how exercise can help the digestive system and the circulatory system.

4. Make a chart to show the benefits of saying no to alcohol, marijuana, and cocaine.

Applying Science

1. Imagine you can see inside the circulatory system. Write a "play-by-play" description—similar to a sportscaster's—telling what happens as blood makes its way through the heart, arteries, capillaries, and veins.

2. Make a list of rules for preventing food poisoning that you could post on the refrigerator at home. Try to write each rule so that any younger family members can understand it. Draw a picture to illustrate each rule.

3. List the different kinds of exercise you got during the past week. Include activities such as walking, bicycling, and doing active chores, as well as playing sports and games. Use what you have written to develop an exercise plan for next week. Plan to be active in some way every day, and plan for vigorous exercise on at least three days. Write how long you will exercise each day. If there are some new kinds of exercise you would like to try, include them in your plan.

Unit D
Performance Review

Body and Health Fair

Using what you learned in this unit, complete one or more of the following activities to be included in a Body and Health Fair. The fair will help students learn more about how various body systems work and how to keep those systems healthy. You may work by yourself or in a group.

Poetry

Imagine that a piece of popcorn could have feelings. How might it feel as it experiences a journey through the digestive system, from the mouth to the small intestine? Put your ideas into a poem or song titled something like "An Incredible Journey" or "What a Trip!" Plan to recite your poem or sing your song at the fair.

Graph

Measure and record your pulse several different times during one day. For example, measure it before you get out of bed, just after walking to school, while working at your desk, just after playing an active game, and while watching an exciting TV show. Show the results in a graph. Display the graph at the fair. Be prepared to offer explanations for any differences in your heart rate that the graph shows.

Drama

Plan a puppet show starring Harry the Heart and Susie the Stomach. Make a hand puppet to represent each character. Prepare a script in which Harry and Susie talk about their jobs, how their owners treat them, and how they wish they could treated. Present your puppet show at the fair. You may want to include recorded music, props, scenery, or special lighting in your show.

Research Report

Find out about animals that help people who are vision impaired and hearing impaired. Prepare a display about these animals for the fair. Your display might include photographs that you have taken, drawings you have made, or copies of pictures from books and magazines. Write descriptive labels for the various pictures. Include information about the animals' training and their daily lives with the people they help.

Health and Safety

You have been named safety officer for your school. Make one or more safety posters to present at the fair. Think of some slogans for staying safe while at school and while traveling to and from school. Include ideas for preventing cuts and head, eye, and ear injuries. Illustrate your safety slogans with pictures that you draw or cut out of old magazines.

D 63

Writing for Science

Writing an Adventure Story or Play

An adventure story or play is an entertaining way to present information. To tell a good story, you need to put events in a logical order and create interesting characters.

Using Graphic Organizers

A graphic organizer is a visual device that helps make facts and ideas clearer. Word webs, flowcharts, and tables are different kinds of graphic organizers. The graphic organizer below is an example of a flowchart. A flowchart shows a series of events in the order in which they occur. This flowchart shows the path of food through your digestive system.

Make a Flowchart

In Chapter 1, you learned about the circulatory system and how blood moves through the heart and body. Use information from Lesson 2 to make a flowchart that traces the path of blood through the human heart.

Write an Adventure Story or Play

Use the information in your flowchart to write an adventure story or play in which the main character is a red blood cell. Your story or play should tell about the main character's adventures as it travels through the human heart. Try to be as descriptive as possible about what the blood cell might experience during this journey.

Remember to:

1. **Prewrite** Organize your thoughts before you write.
2. **Draft** Write your story or play.
3. **Revise** Share your work and then make changes.
4. **Edit** Proofread for mistakes and fix them.
5. **Publish** Share your story or play with your class.

mouth → throat → esophagus → stomach → intestines

Your Science Handbook

⚠️ **Safety in Science**	**2**
Using the Metric System	**4**
Science Process Skills Lessons	
Observing	6
Communicating	8
Classifying	10
Estimating and Measuring	12
Inferring	14
Predicting	16
Making Operational Definitions	18
Making and Using Models	20
Formulating Questions and Hypotheses	22
Collecting and Interpreting Data	24
Identifying and Controlling Variables	26
Experimenting	28
Science Reference Section	**30**
Ⓗ **History of Science**	**48**
Glossary	**60**
Index	**70**

⚠️ Safety in Science

Scientists know they must work safely when doing experiments. You need to be careful when doing experiments too. The next page shows some safety tips to remember.

Safety Tips

- Read each experiment carefully.
- Wear safety goggles when needed.
- Clean up spills right away.
- Never taste or smell substances unless directed to do so by your teacher.
- Handle sharp items carefully.
- Tape sharp edges of materials.
- Handle thermometers carefully.
- Use chemicals carefully.
- Dispose of chemicals properly.
- Put materials away when you finish an experiment.
- Wash your hands after each experiment.

Using the Metric System

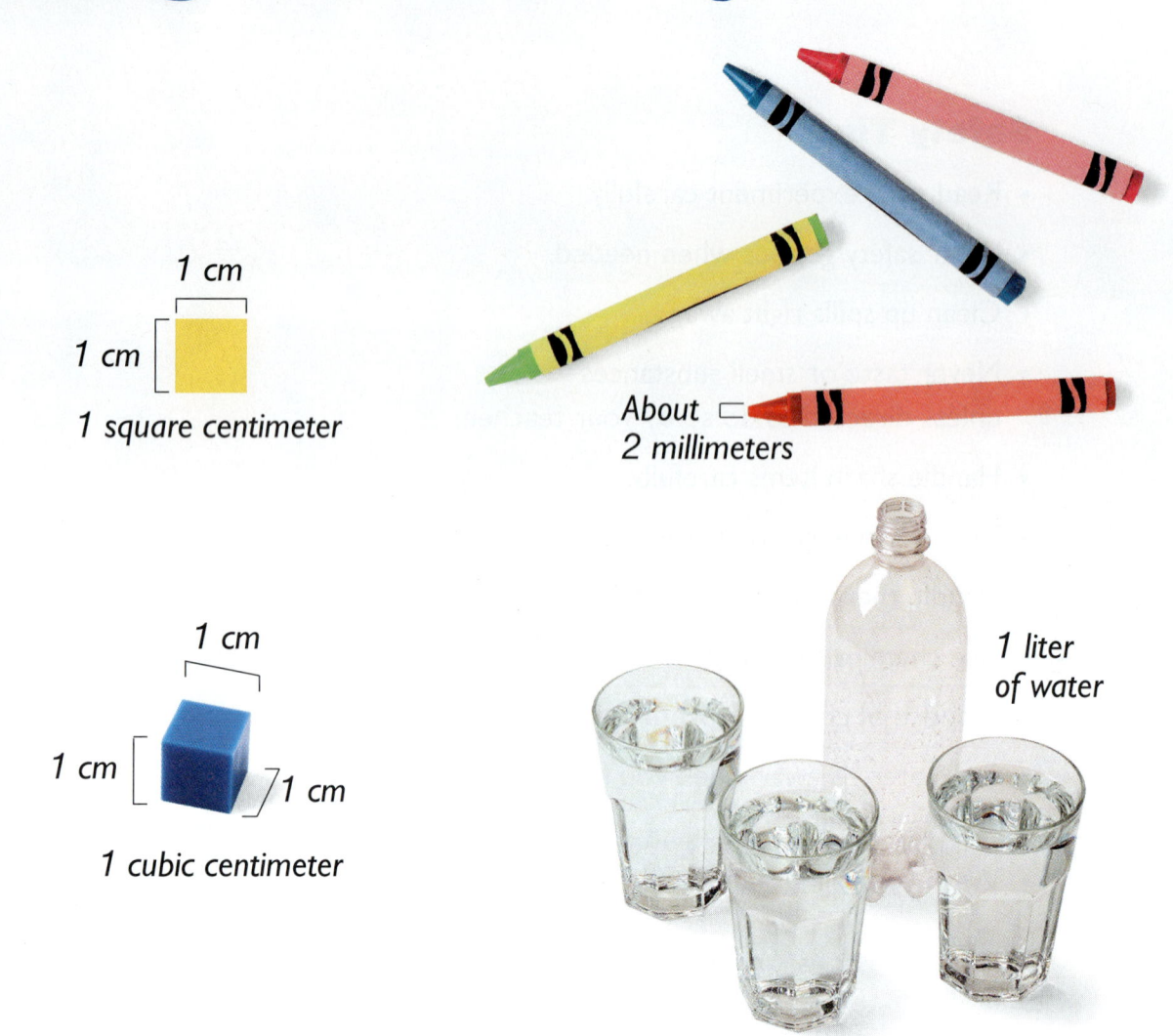

1 cm
1 cm
1 square centimeter

About 2 millimeters

1 cm
1 cm
1 cm
1 cubic centimeter

1 liter of water

11 football fields end to end is about 1 kilometer

About 1 centimeter

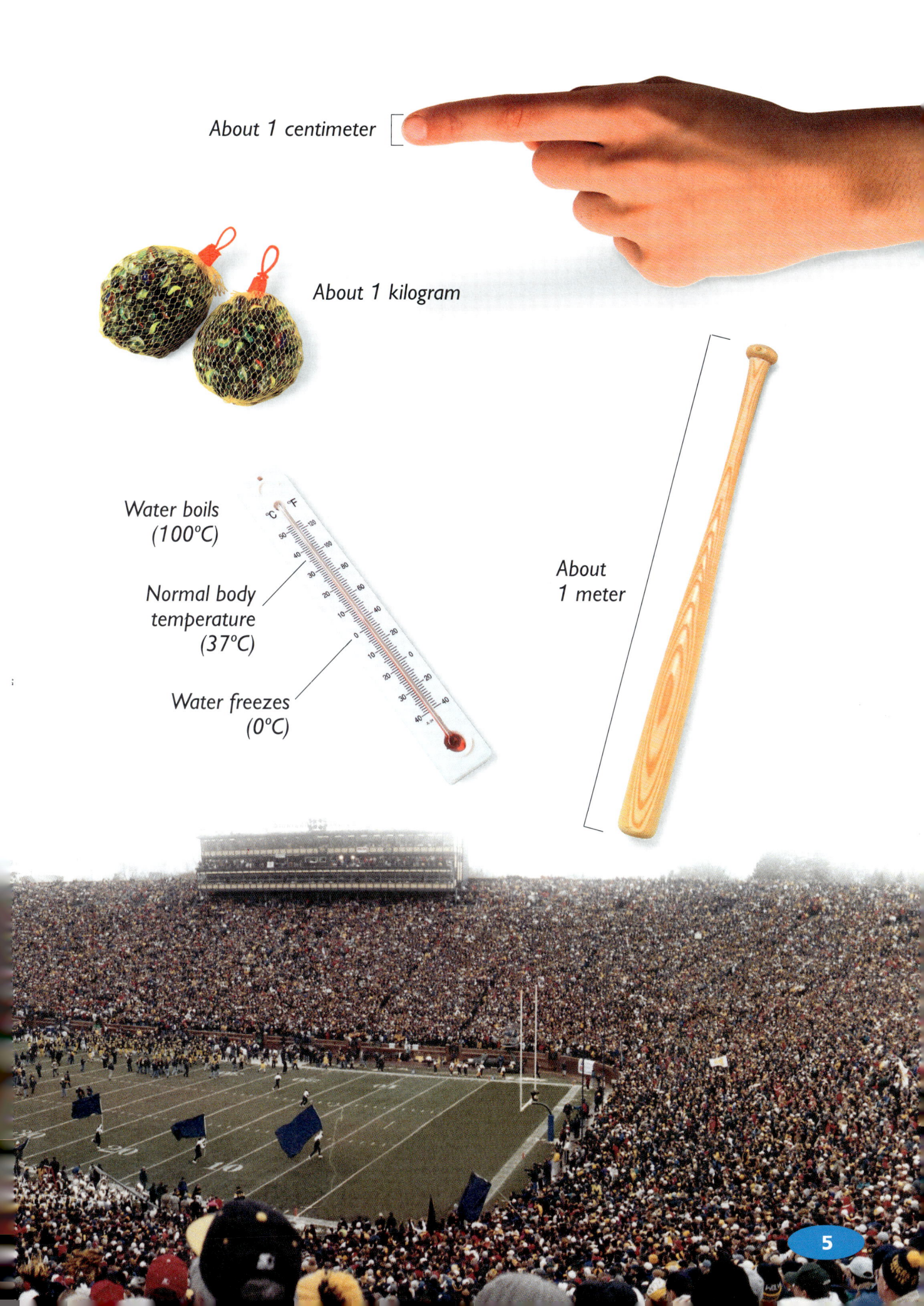

About 1 kilogram

Water boils (100°C)

Normal body temperature (37°C)

Water freezes (0°C)

About 1 meter

Science Process Skill

Observing

How can you make accurate observations?

The process of observing is the most important of all the process skills. Every scientific investigation requires you to make accurate observations.

You must use all your senses—sight, touch, hearing, smelling, and taste—to find out about objects and events. You can pick up objects, feel them, shake them, press them, smell them, look at them, listen to them. Doing all these things will help you find out about objects.

Observing requires that you notice things or events that are changing. You must compare the properties of the objects or events before, during, and after the change.

You may use tools or measuring instruments to make better observations. Limit your observations to things that are directly related to your senses.

Practice Observing

Materials
- pencil
- paper
- tape measure
- hand lens

Follow This Procedure

1. Observe your pencil with as many senses as possible. Do not taste your pencil.

2. List each sense that you used and list your observations.

3. Notice things that are changing. Compare properties before, during, and after the change. For example, use your hand lens to look carefully at the "lead" in your pencil. It is graphite. Then scribble on a piece of paper. Describe how the graphite looked before, during, and after you scribbled on the paper.

4. Use tools to make better observations. Use a tape measure to make observations of your pencil. Make as many measurements as you can.

5. Describe only what you observe directly with your senses. Look over your list of observations and tell what sense you used to make each observation.

Thinking About Your Thinking

List the steps that you used to make accurate observations. What could you have done to make better observations?

Science Process Skill

Communicating

How can you communicate by using descriptions?

You communicate when you share information through words, pictures, charts, graphs, and diagrams. Each of these is a different way to communicate.

If you want to communicate about something that has many things to describe, you can use several different ways to express your observations. For example, you might make a map like the one shown. The map shows how to locate a treasure that is hidden on the island in the picture.

Practice Communicating

Materials
- ruler
- pencil
- notebook

Follow This Procedure

1. Begin a letter to a friend from another school, telling him or her that you will be describing your classroom.

2. Describe the light in the classroom. Is it mostly from the windows? What time of day is the window light brightest? Are there ceiling lights?

3. Describe the smell of the air. Does it smell like an old shoe? like flowers? like mouthwash?

4. Describe the color and texture of the walls. Does tape stick to it? Is the floor rough or smooth? Is it slippery?

5. Draw a map of the classroom. Include the doors, windows, blackboards, desks, and closets. Draw and label any special activity areas. Label your assigned seat if you have one.

6. Measure and describe the classroom by the "steps" method. First measure the length of your step in centimeters. Count how many steps it takes to cross the length of the classroom. Then count how many steps it takes to cross the width. Calculate the length of the classroom by multiplying the length of your steps by the number of steps necessary to cross its length. Use the same calculation to find the width. Record your results. In the letter you are writing, describe how your measurements were obtained.

7. Compare your letter with the letter of another student to discover what you may not have communicated.

Thinking About Your Thinking

How did creating a map improve the communication in your letter? Could you have described a complex environment like your classroom as well without it? Would it have taken a lot more words?

Think about how important it is for people to communicate the methods and units of measurement they are using. Is the "steps" method precise enough to communicate how to build parts for an airplane? What other ways to measure might you have used?

Science Process Skill

Classifying

How can you classify objects in nature?

You classify objects by arranging or grouping them according to their common properties. Practice classifying things in nature. It is important to use an organized way to classify.

Look at the leaves on this page. How are these leaves alike and different? How would you group these leaves according to their common properties?

Practice Classifying

Materials
- collection of six leaves
- small magnifying glass
- pencil

Follow This Procedure

1. Classify your collection of leaves by their different characteristics. Make a list of the characteristics you used.

2. How many different ways did you sort your collection? Why did you choose those characteristics?

3. Plant scientists, or botanists, classify leaves in many ways. Look at each of your leaves. Are they thin and needle-like? Are they broad, or wide?

4. Look at a broad leaf. Notice the little stem at the bottom. The rest of the leaf is called the *blade*. Veins run from the little stem into the blade. You can see them with or without your hand lens. Do the veins alternate off of one big vein in the middle? Do they all branch off from the stem? Do they run in straight lines without touching?

5. Classify your broad leaves as one of the following.

    (1) having alternating veins
    (2) having branching veins
    (3) going in a straight line

Thinking About Your Thinking

Would you have thought about classifying leaves by their vein structure?

How else could you classify leaves? Could you have used color pattern? smell?

Science Process Skill

Estimating and Measuring

How can you estimate and measure a large number of objects?

An estimate is an intelligent, informed guess about an object's properties. Sometimes you may want to estimate how many objects are in a container without having to count or measure every object.

Suppose you were given the assignment to tell how many raisins were in a box of cereal. You surely wouldn't want to count every raisin. That would take too long. Instead you could decide on a plan to estimate and measure the cereal to come up with a reasonable answer.

Practice Estimating and Measuring

Materials
- 16 oz. box of raisin cereal
- measuring cup
- large bowl

Follow This Procedure

1. Work with a partner to estimate the number of raisins in the box of cereal.

2. Use the measuring cup to determine how many cups of cereal are in the box. Pour the cereal into the measuring cup and then put the cereal from the measuring cup into the bowl. Keep track of how many cups you poured into the bowl.

3. Divide the total number of cups in the box by 2. Round the answer up to the next whole number. Write down this number.

4. Use the measuring cup to take 2 cups of cereal back out of the bowl. Separate the raisins from the cereal. Count how many raisins were in the two cups of cereal.

5. Multiply the number of raisins in two cups of cereal by the number that you got in step 3. This will give you an estimate of the number of raisins in the whole box of cereal.

Thinking About Your Thinking

Can you think of another way to make a better estimate of the number of raisins in the box? Would taking a larger sample of cereal make any difference to the accuracy of your estimate? Try it to find out.

Science Process Skill

STAY HEALTHY!
Drink Orange Juice

Orange juice is good and it's good for you!

Get the— Vitamin C, Fiber, and Potassium that you need!

Inferring

How do you infer?

You infer when you make a reasonable guess, based on what you observe or on what you have experienced.

Observing with one or more of your senses—seeing, hearing, smelling, or touching—can be the reason for your inference. If you have done something in the past, what you learned can also help you make a good inference.

For example, when you watch TV or read a magazine, there are commercials or ads. You have seen these before and you know that someone is trying to sell you something. Watch a commercial. What do the advertisers want you to believe about their product?

Ad	Observation	Inference

Practice Inferring

Materials
- magazines or newspapers

Follow This Procedure

1. Make a chart like the one shown.

2. Look through a magazine or newspaper. Cut out several ads.

3. Read these ads carefully. List an observation and an inference that could be made about the ad.

4. Draw a conclusion about these ads. Is the message that the advertiser was trying to send accurate? Why or why not?

Thinking About Your Thinking

Watch several commercials on television. How do the commercials compare to the ads in the magazine or newspaper? Which type of advertising is more likely to make you want to buy a product—ads or TV commercials? Why do you think this is so?

Science Process Skill

Predicting

How can you make accurate predictions?

Predicting is an important process skill. There are five steps to making accurate predictions.

1. Make observations and measurements. Remember what you learned from doing something in the past.
2. Search for patterns in the data. Make inferences.
3. Make predictions about what may happen in the future. Use your inferences.
4. Test your predictions.
5. After testing, revise your predictions if necessary.

Practice Predicting

Materials
- meter stick
- small rubber ball

Follow This Procedure

1 Make a chart like the one below.

Drop	Predictions	Bounces
25 cm	X	
30 cm	X	
50 cm		
75 cm		
100 cm		

2 Work with a partner. Have your partner hold the meter stick with the 100 cm at the top.

3 Drop the ball from the 25 centimeter line on the meter stick. Have your partner count how many times the ball bounces.

4 Repeat this activity from the 30 centimeter line. Record the number of bounces.

5 Predict how many times the ball will bounce from the 50, 75, and 100 centimeter lines.

6 Do the activity and record the number of times the ball bounces from the 50, 75, and 100 centimeter lines.

Thinking About Your Thinking

How accurate were your predictions? What information did you use to make your predictions? If you dropped the ball from 200 centimeters, what would your prediction for the number of bounces be? Why?

Science Process Skill

Making Operational Definitions

How do you write an operational definition?

An operational definition is a definition or description of an object or an event based on your experience with it. As you gain experience with an object or event, your operational definition of it may become more effective. Keep your operational definition as simple as possible. Can you write an operational definition for the word "electricity"? Remember, use what you know already to write the definition. Do not look it up in a dictionary.

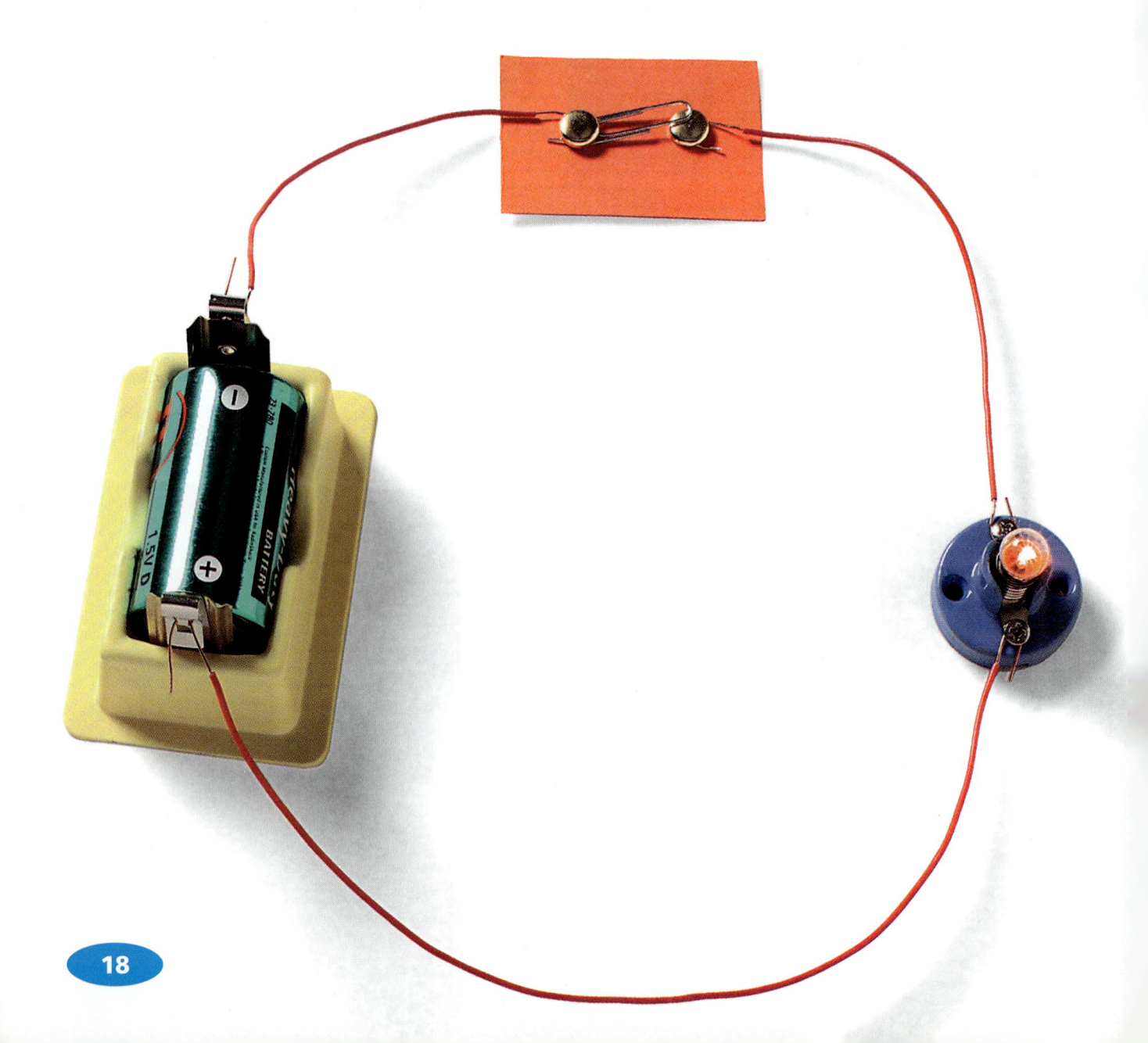

Practice Making Operational Definitions

Materials
- 1 D-cell battery
- 1 flashlight bulb
- insulated wire—both ends stripped

Follow This Procedure

1. Look at the diagram of the closed circuit. Set up the bulb, battery, and wire to make a closed circuit so the bulb lights.

2. Write your definition of a closed circuit based on what you did.

3. Look up *circuit* in your science book or the dictionary and write the definition given in the book.

4. How is your definition of a circuit different from the definition given in the book?

Thinking About Your Thinking

How did making a closed circuit help you define it? How did your definition communicate what the closed circuit did?

Science Process Skill

Making and Using Models

How can making a model help you understand a difficult concept?

There are many things to learn in your science book. Some of those things are easier to understand if you can see the object or event. You can make a model or copy of many of the objects or events in science.

For example, you can't go to a desert, forest, or prairie to see how animals live in these environments. However, you can build dioramas in shoeboxes or make posters of animals in their habitats. These models help you learn about animals and their habitats.

Practice Making and Using Models

Materials

- clear tape
- pictures of animals from magazines, web sites, or student drawings
- 4 different pieces of construction paper
- large poster board

Follow This Procedure

1. Cut out or draw pictures of 4 animals that go together in a food chain.
2. Tape these animals on the 4 different pieces of construction paper.
3. Put the pictures in order on the poster board.
4. Label the food chain, showing the direction that it goes.
5. Write a description of the food chain that you created for your class.
6. Create a series of questions that go with your food chain. Have your classmates answer these questions. Examples might be:

   What is the source of energy for the ____?

   What does the ____ eat?

   Which animal or organism starts the food chain?

   What do you think would happen to the ____ if it couldn't eat the ____?

Thinking About Your Thinking

Why do you think that the model that you made is called a "chain"? What other models could you make that might help explain what a food chain is?

Science Process Skill

Formulating Questions and Hypotheses

How do you formulate relevant questions and hypotheses?

The scientific process often begins when you ask yourself a question to solve a problem. You then formulate statements, or hypotheses, so you can test them. From the results of the test, you may be able to answer the question or to solve the problem.

When scientists form a possible answer to a question, they also form a hypothesis. For example, "If I do this ... then this will happen."

Practice Formulating Questions and Hypotheses

Materials
- 6 straws
- scissors
- tape
- piece of construction paper

Follow This Procedure

1. Question: How does the length of the straw affect the pitch of the sound produced?

2. Cut one end of a straw to form a point and blow into this end of the straw to produce a sound. Observe the pitch of the sound produced (high or low).

3. Write a hypothesis about the length of the straw and its pitch.

4. Trim the 5 remaining straws to different lengths. Then cut one end of each straw to form a point. Blow into this end and observe the pitch of the sound produced.

5. Arrange your 6 straws in order from the highest to the lowest pitch and tape the straws on a piece of construction paper.

Thinking About Your Thinking

Did your investigation prove that your hypothesis is correct?

As you observe at school and home, think about questions you would like to find out about. Practice forming hypotheses to answer your questions. How would you test each hypothesis?

Science Process Skill

Collecting and Interpreting Data

How do you collect and interpret data accurately?

You collect and interpret data when you gather measurements and organize them into graphs, tables, charts, or diagrams. You can then use the information to solve problems or to answer questions.

When people take surveys, they ask many questions and collect a lot of useful data. This information is then put into charts and graphs so it's easier to understand. Have you ever taken a survey?

1. What color eyes do you have? _____

2. What color hair do you have? _____

3. How many brothers and sisters do you have? _____

Practice Collecting and Interpreting Data

Materials
- pencil
- paper

Follow This Procedure

1 Make a chart like the one below to record how many of your classmates have blue eyes, brown eyes, or green eyes.

Eye Color	Tally of Students	Totals
Blue		
Brown		
Green		

2 Make a chart like the one below to record how many of your classmates have blonde hair, red hair, brown hair, or black hair.

Hair Color	Tally of Students	Totals
Blonde		
Red		
Brown		
Black		

3 Take a survey to collect data on hair color and eye color from each of your classmates. Make a tally mark for each student's answer in the correct place on the charts. Then calculate the total number of students that chose each answer.

4 Which hair color do most students have? Which eye color do most students have?

Thinking About Your Thinking

What other questions might you have included on your survey? Is a chart the best way to show this data? Why or why not?

Science Process Skill

Identifying and Controlling Variables

How do you identify and control variables?

You identify and control variables when you change one factor that may affect the outcome of an event while keeping all other factors the same.

The first step is to determine which variable you want to change. You must also identify the variables you want to keep the same.

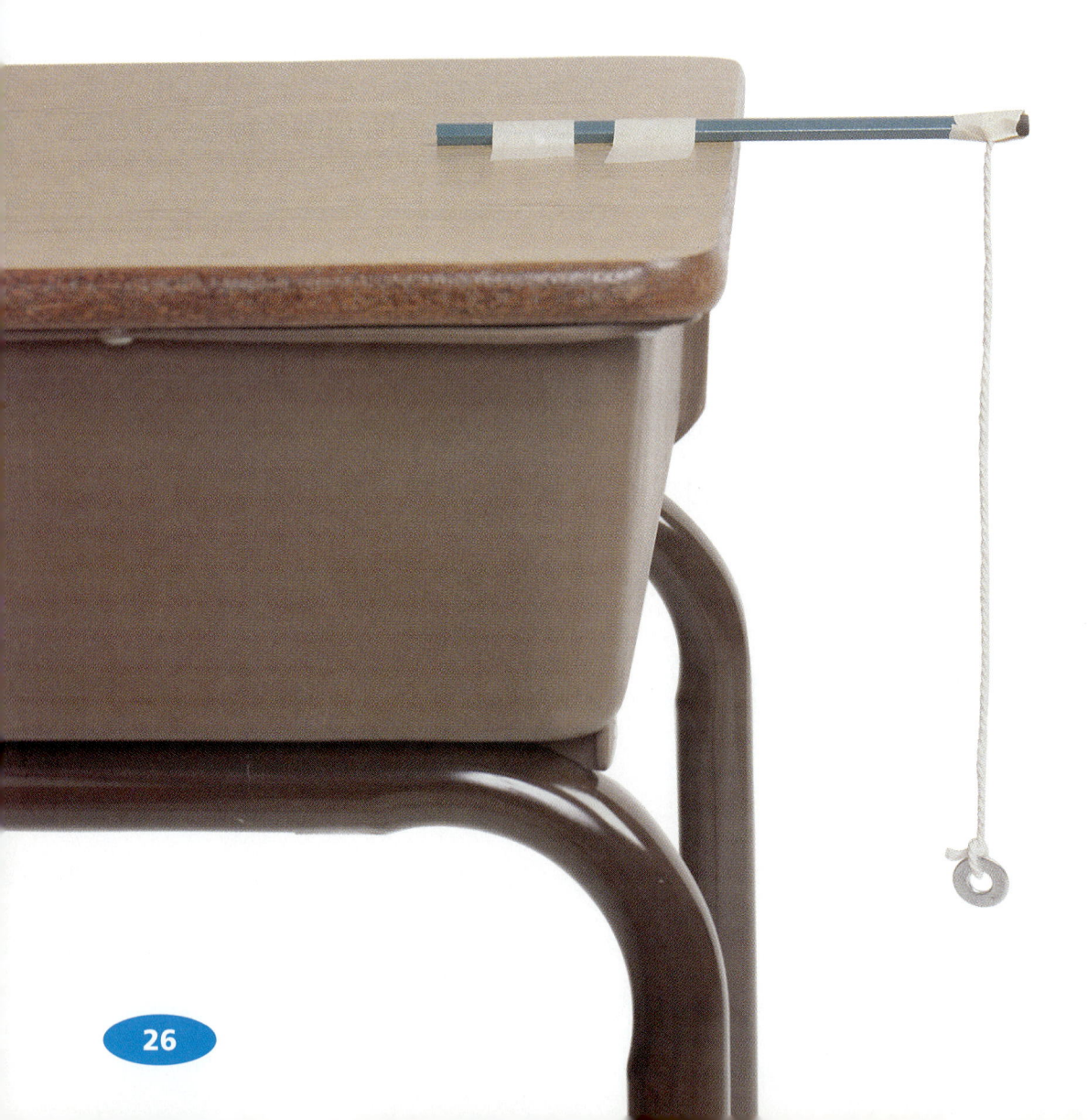

Practice Identifying and Controlling Variables

Materials
- string
- scissors
- metric ruler
- 6 washers
- pencil
- tape
- timer or watch with second hand

Follow This Procedure

1. Make a chart like the one below.

Length of Pendulum	Number of Swings
60 cm	
50 cm	
40 cm	
30 cm	
20 cm	
10 cm	

2. Cut the string into 6 pieces of the following lengths: 60 cm, 50 cm, 40 cm, 30 cm, 20 cm, 10 cm. Tie a washer to the end of each piece of string.

3. Tape the pencil to the table so that about 3 cm hangs over the edge. Tape the 60 cm pendulum onto the pencil. Hold the washer even with the top of the table and release it.

4. Count how many times the pendulum swings back and forth in 15 seconds, and record the number of swings in the chart.

5. Repeat this procedure with the other five pendulums.

Thinking About Your Thinking

Which variable did you change? Which variable responded to the change (what did you count)? Which variables were kept constant? How does the length of the pendulum affect the number of times it swings in 15 seconds?

Science Process Skill

Experimenting

What does scientific experimenting involve?

Scientific experimenting involves making a plan to test a hypothesis and then forming a conclusion based on the results.

The first step is to write the problem you are investigating and come up with a hypothesis.

Next, think how you should organize, or design, the investigation. Which variables will you keep constant? What one variable will you decide to change?

Next, perform the experiment to test your hypothesis. Accurate record keeping is another important part of experimenting. You should record your procedure and data accurately so that you and others can repeat the experiment.

Practice Experimenting

Materials
- masking tape
- magnets of different strengths
- paper clips

Follow This Procedure

1. Use the masking tape to label the magnets *1* and *2*. Look at the two magnets. Can you tell which magnet will pick up the most paper clips?

2. State the problem. Which magnet is stronger?

3. Write a hypothesis about which magnet you think will pick up more paper clips.

4. Design your experiment. The variable that changes is the magnet. Are the paper clips a variable that changes?

5. Construct a chart like the one below to show your results.

Number of Paper Clips Picked Up	
Magnet 1	
Magnet 2	

6. Perform the experiment.

7. Make a grid for a bar graph like the one below. Graph your results.

8. Compare your hypothesis with the results. State your conclusion.

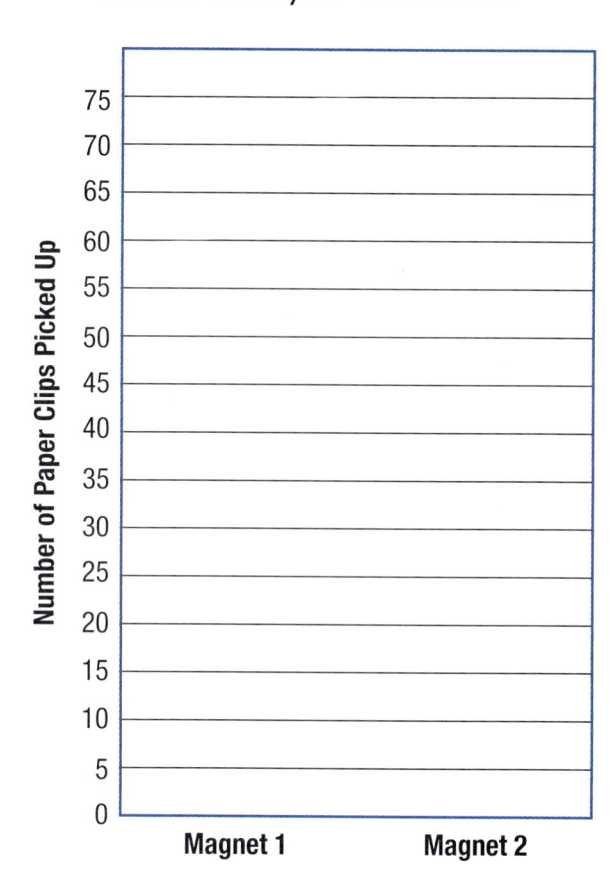

Thinking About Your Thinking

What did you learn from this experiment?

29

Science Reference Section

Systems

A system is a set of things that form a whole. Systems can be made of many different parts. All the parts depend on each other and work together. Systems can have living things and nonliving things.

The schoolyard on the next page is an example of a system that contains living things. Parts of the system that interact and depend on each other are the students, the grass, the bee, the clover plant, and the dandelion plant.

The circuit below is a nonliving system. The light bulb, the wires, the switch, and the energy source all make up the system.

31

Layers of the Earth

Atmosphere
A blanket of air, called the atmosphere, surrounds the earth. The earth's atmosphere protects it from harmful sunlight and helps organisms on the earth survive.

Crust
The earth itself is made of layers. The outer layer, or crust, of the earth is made up of rocks and soil. The land you walk on and the land under the oceans are part of the crust.

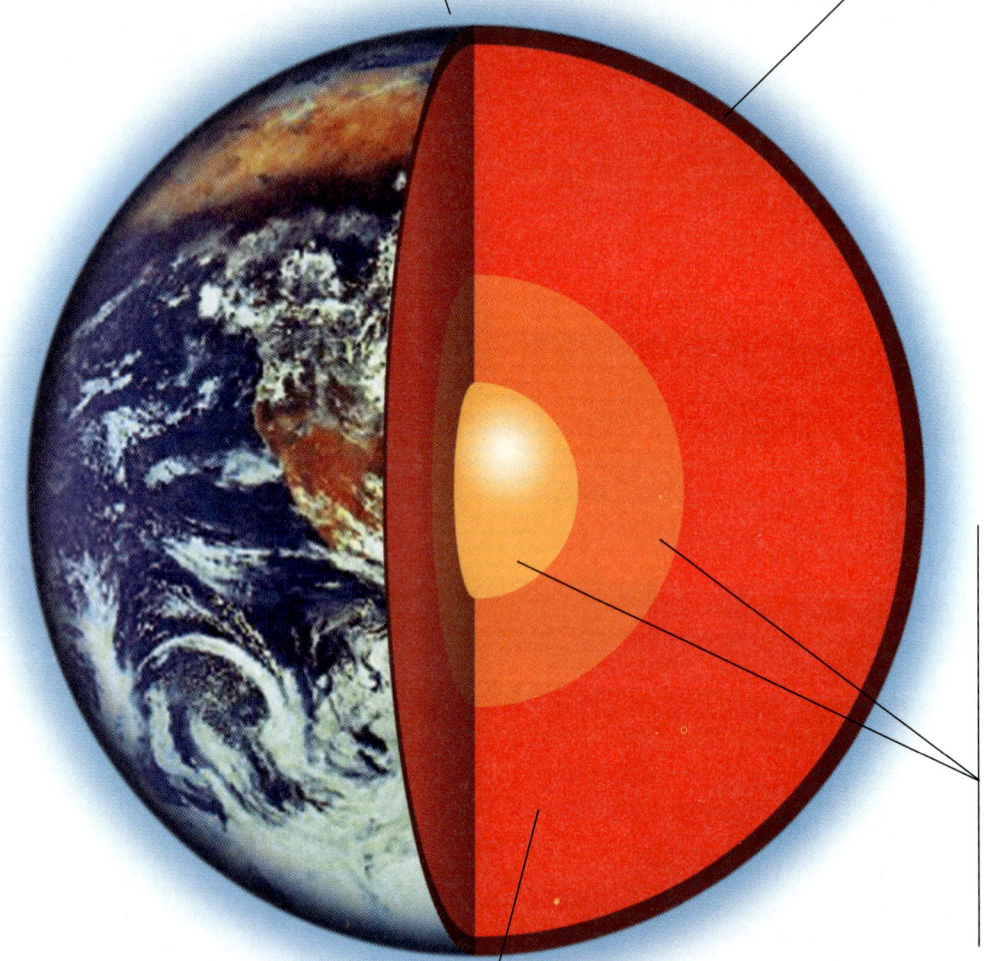

Core
The center of the earth—the core—is made mostly of iron. The outside part of the core has liquid iron. The inside part has solid iron. The core is the hottest part of the earth. The temperature of the core is almost as hot as the surface of the sun!

Mantle
The middle layer of the earth is called the mantle. The mantle is mostly made of rock. Some of the rock in the mantle is partly melted.

Climate Zones

A climate is the weather conditions which describe an area over many years. The earth has three basic climate zones—tropical, temperate, and polar. Areas within these zones can have different climates. Across the United States, climates vary because of differences in the amount of rainfall and temperature. There are no clear boundary lines between climate areas in the United States.

Highland climate
The highland climate mountain zones have very cold winters and cool summers.

Grassland climate
A grassland climate gets little rainfall during the year. This zone has very cold temperatures and snow in winter and hot temperatures in the summer.

Humid continental climate
A humid continental climate has warm summers with a lot of rain. Winters are very cold with a lot of snow.

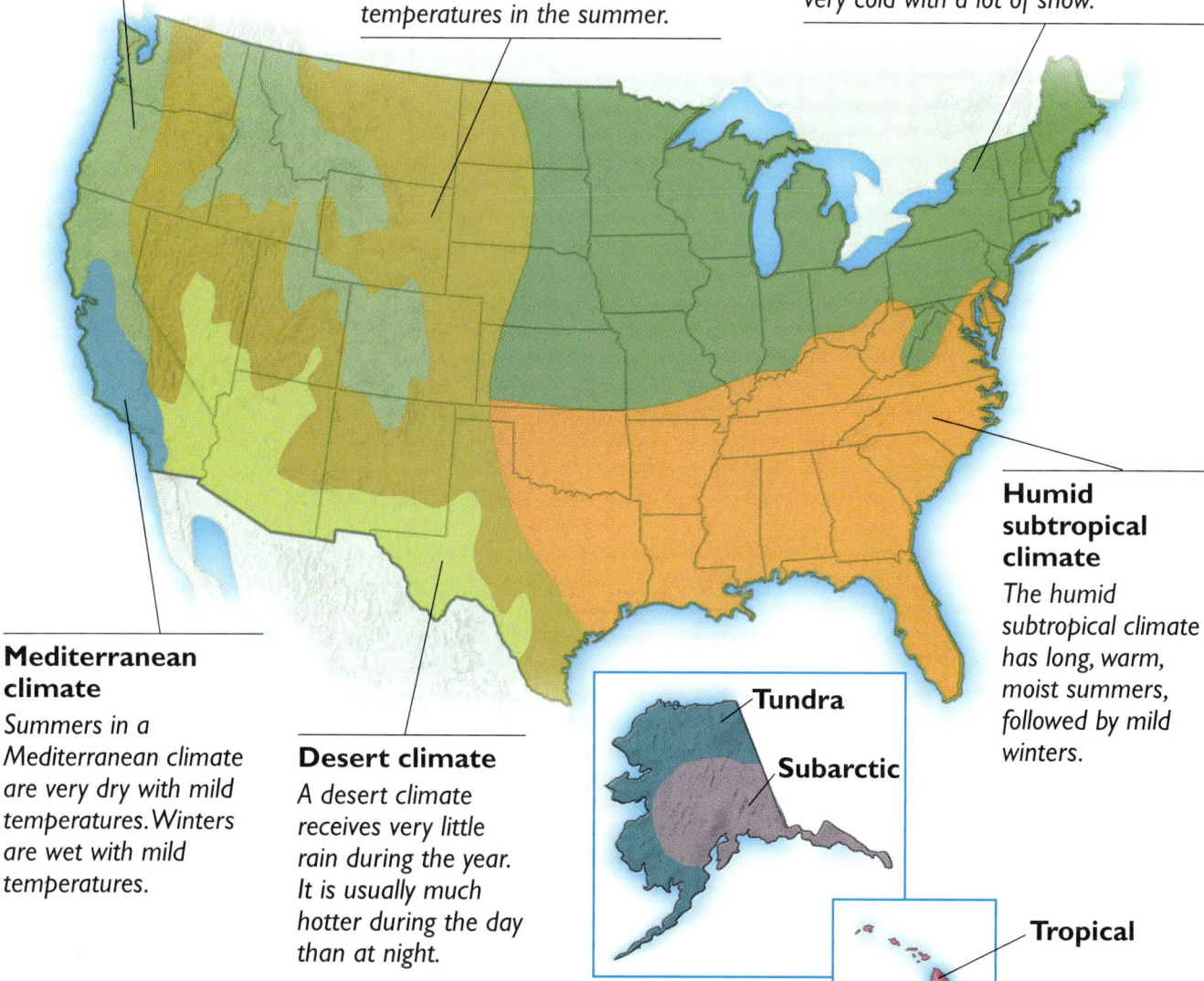

Humid subtropical climate
The humid subtropical climate has long, warm, moist summers, followed by mild winters.

Mediterranean climate
Summers in a Mediterranean climate are very dry with mild temperatures. Winters are wet with mild temperatures.

Desert climate
A desert climate receives very little rain during the year. It is usually much hotter during the day than at night.

Tundra

Subarctic

Tropical

The Rock Cycle

In the rock cycle, rocks form and change into other types of rock. Rocks form in three main ways. Over millions of years, each type of rock can change into another type of rock.

Rocks that form from melted material deep inside the earth are igneous rocks. Granite is an igneous rock.

As a result of weathering, rocks break down. Sand and small bits of rock sink beneath the water. Layers of material press together underwater and form sedimentary rocks. Sandstone is a sedimentary rock.

Metamorphic rock forms as very high heat and great pressure within the earth change igneous and sedimentary rocks. Gneiss is a metamorphic rock.

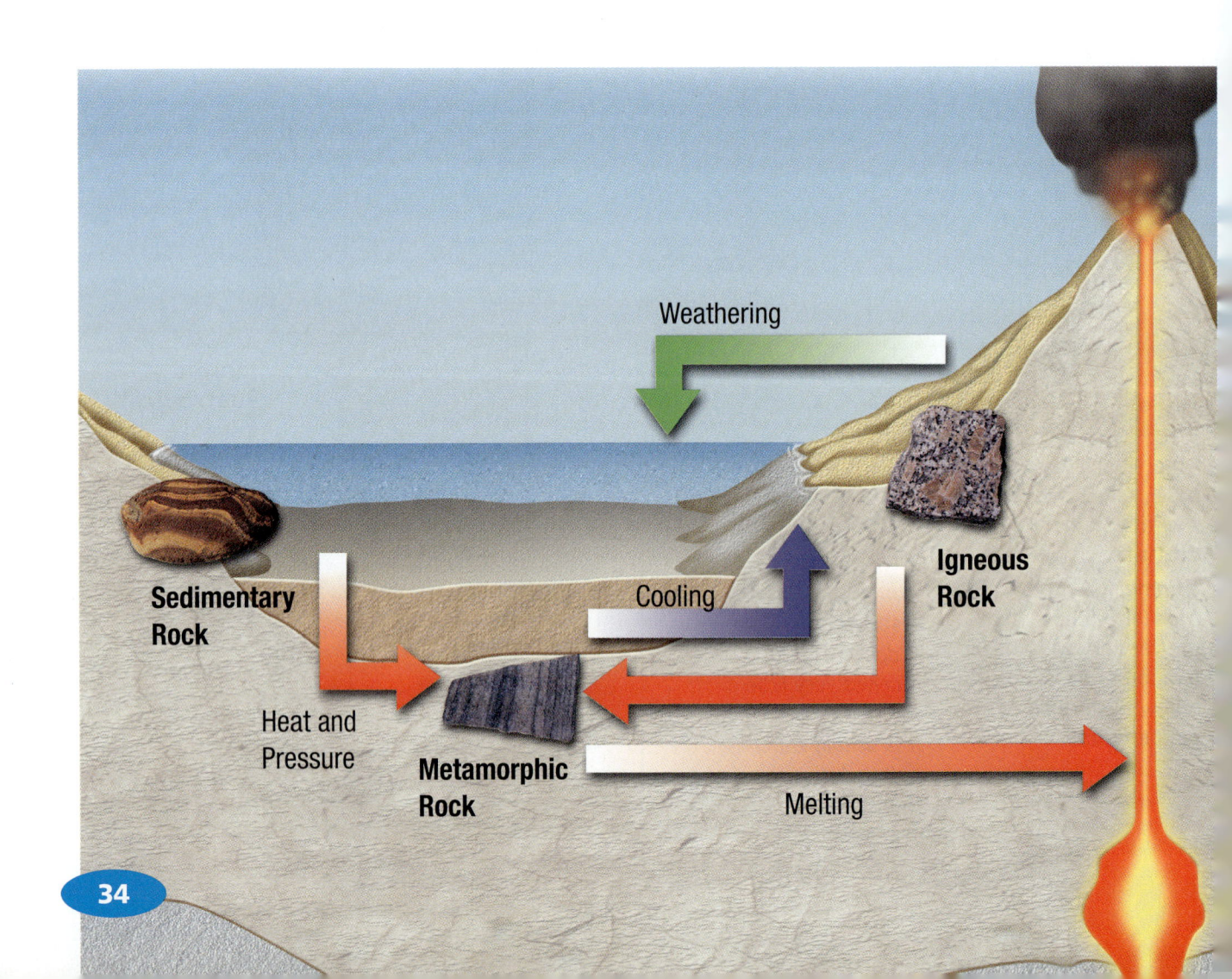

Minerals

In 1822, Frederich Mohs created a scale that showed the hardness of certain minerals. On his scale, minerals with higher numbers are harder than minerals with lower numbers. You can tell how hard a mineral is by rubbing it against another mineral. The harder mineral will scratch the softer mineral. A diamond is the hardest mineral known. It will scratch any other mineral.

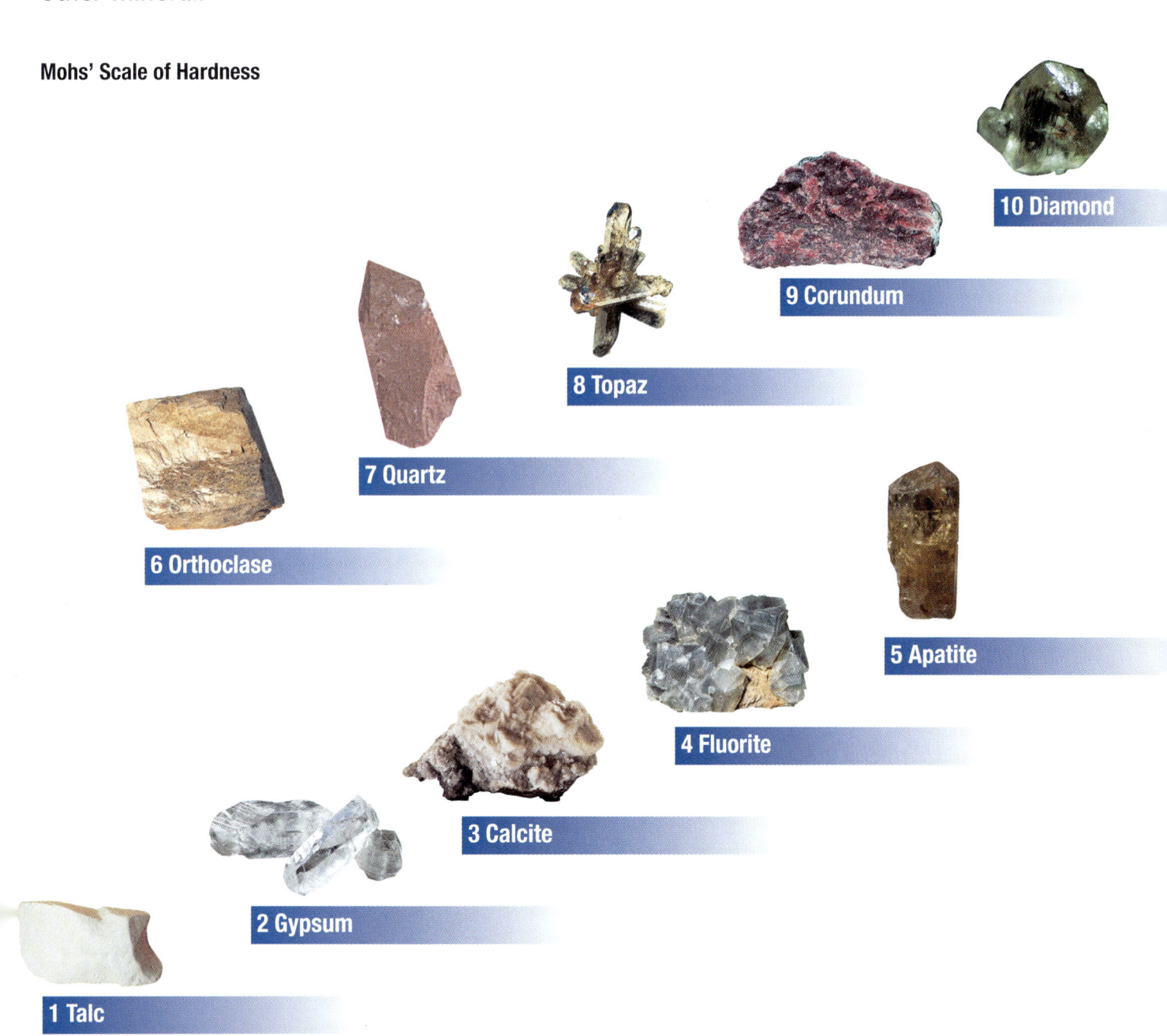

Mohs' Scale of Hardness

10 Diamond
9 Corundum
8 Topaz
7 Quartz
6 Orthoclase
5 Apatite
4 Fluorite
3 Calcite
2 Gypsum
1 Talc

Evidence of the Past

Many different types of organisms have existed on the earth throughout millions of years. Many types of organisms that lived millions of years ago are now extinct. Fossils of extinct organisms show that some plants and animals that lived long ago look very much like plants and animals that live today.

▲ The woolly mammoth from thousands of years ago is similar to the elephant of today. The mammoth is now extinct.

◀ Scientists think that ferns date back hundreds of millions of years, making them some of the oldest types of plants on the earth.

◀ In many ways, a tiger that lives today looks like a saber-toothed cat that lived thousands of years ago. The saber-toothed cat is now extinct.

◀ Cockroaches have been on the earth many millions of years. They look much the same now as their ancestors that lived long ago.

▲ Alligators that lived many millions of years ago may have been longer than alligators that live today. However, ancient alligators looked very much like alligators that live today.

Vertebrates and Invertebrates

The animal kingdom can be divided into two main groups. One group contains animals that have a backbone. Animals that have backbones are called vertebrates. The other group contains animals that do not have a backbone. These animals are called invertebrates.

▲ Crabs belong to a group called crustaceans.

Invertebrates

Earthworms are annelids. ▼

Spiders belong to a group of invertebrates called arachnids. ▶

The group to which sponges belong is known as porifera. ▼

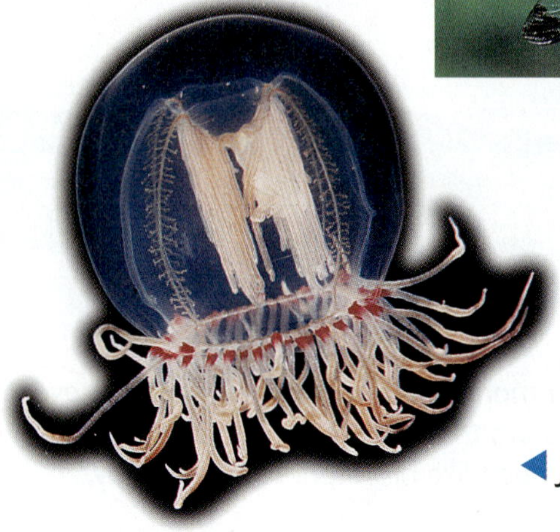

▲ Insects are the largest group of animals.

◀ Jellyfish are coelenterates.

Vertebrates

◀ *Snakes, turtles, and lizards belong to a group called reptiles.*

▲ *A hummingbird is one of many different birds.*

Koalas are mammals. ▶

Frogs are amphibians. ▶

Sharks are fishes. ▶

Life Cycles

Every living thing has a life cycle. In its life cycle, an organism goes through stages in which it grows, changes, and reproduces. Some young animals have the same body form as their parents. Others, such as frogs and butterflies, go through a metamorphosis, meaning they change form as they grow.

Life Cycle of a Frog

Frog eggs
Frogs lay eggs in water.

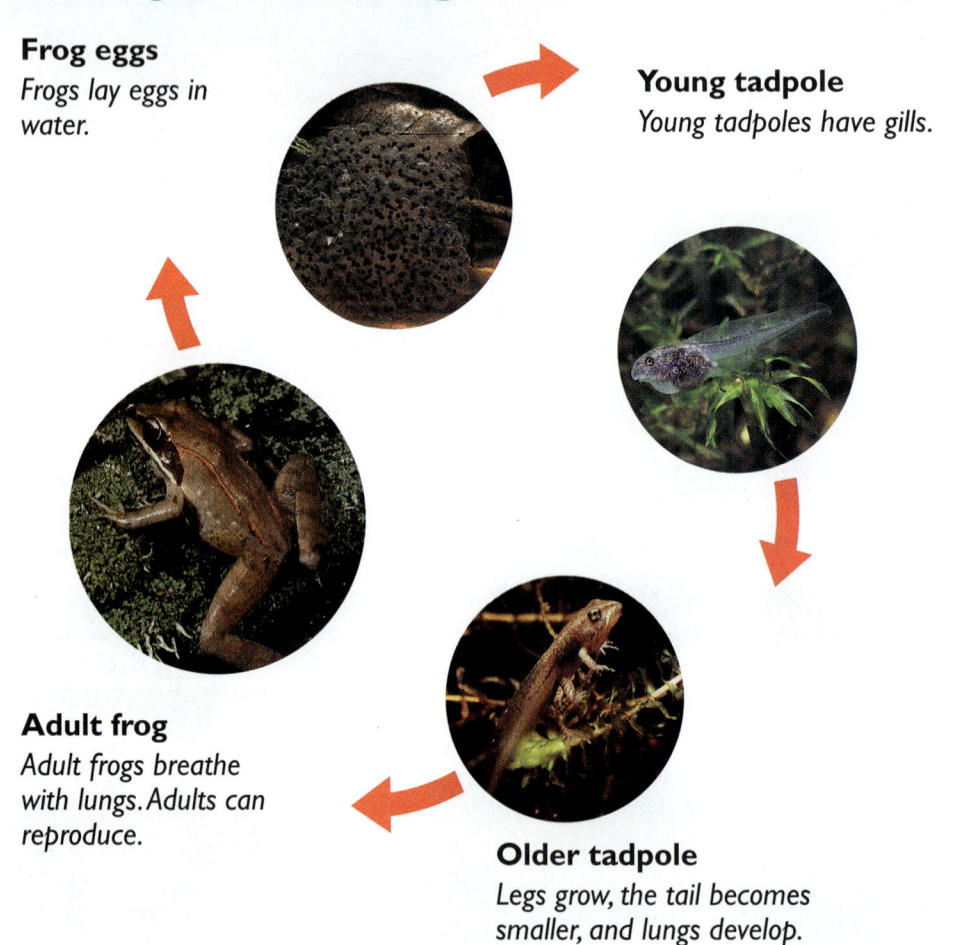

Young tadpole
Young tadpoles have gills.

Older tadpole
Legs grow, the tail becomes smaller, and lungs develop.

Adult frog
Adult frogs breathe with lungs. Adults can reproduce.

Life Cycle of a Butterfly

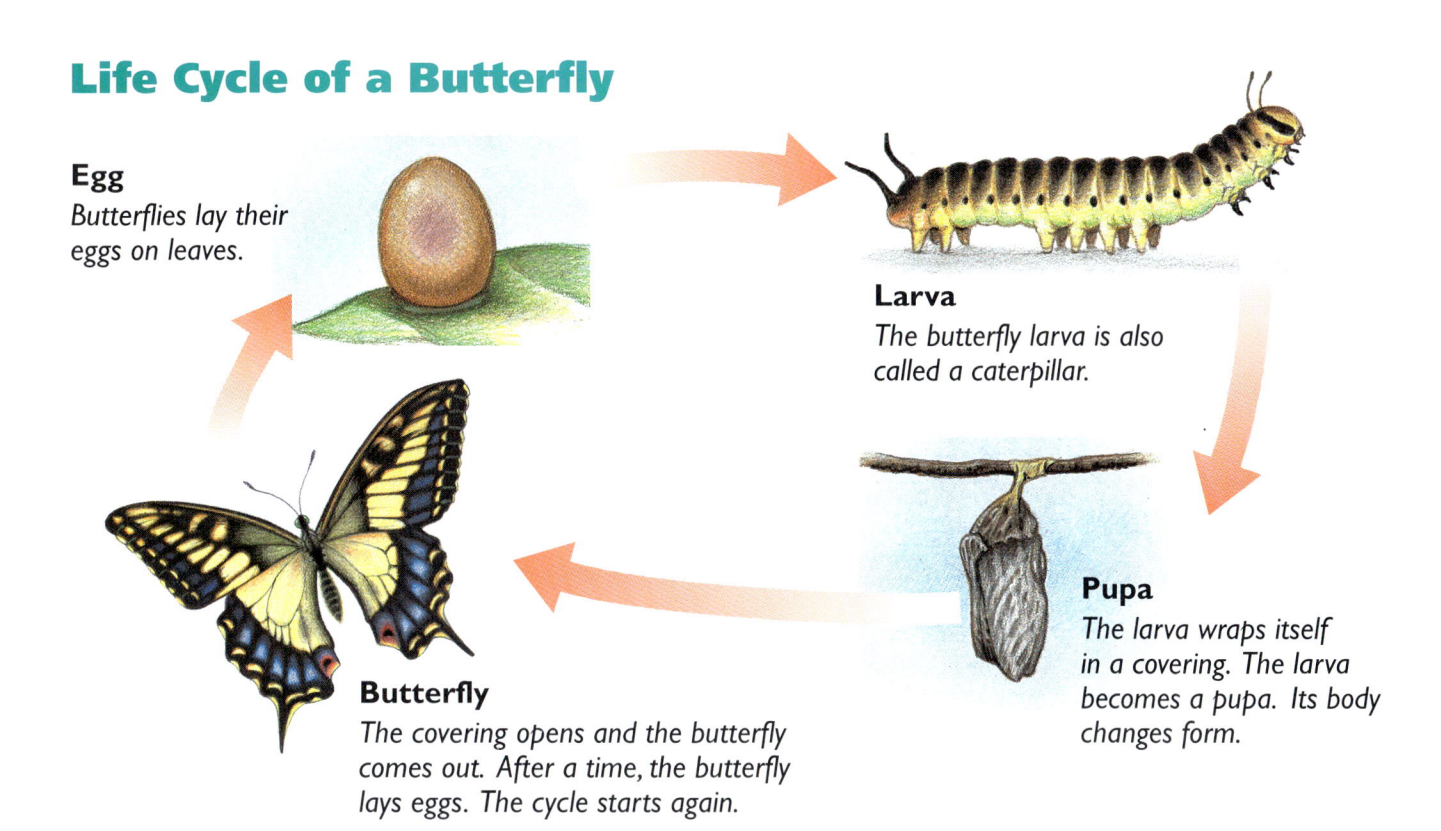

Egg
Butterflies lay their eggs on leaves.

Larva
The butterfly larva is also called a caterpillar.

Pupa
The larva wraps itself in a covering. The larva becomes a pupa. Its body changes form.

Butterfly
The covering opens and the butterfly comes out. After a time, the butterfly lays eggs. The cycle starts again.

Life Cycle of a Tree

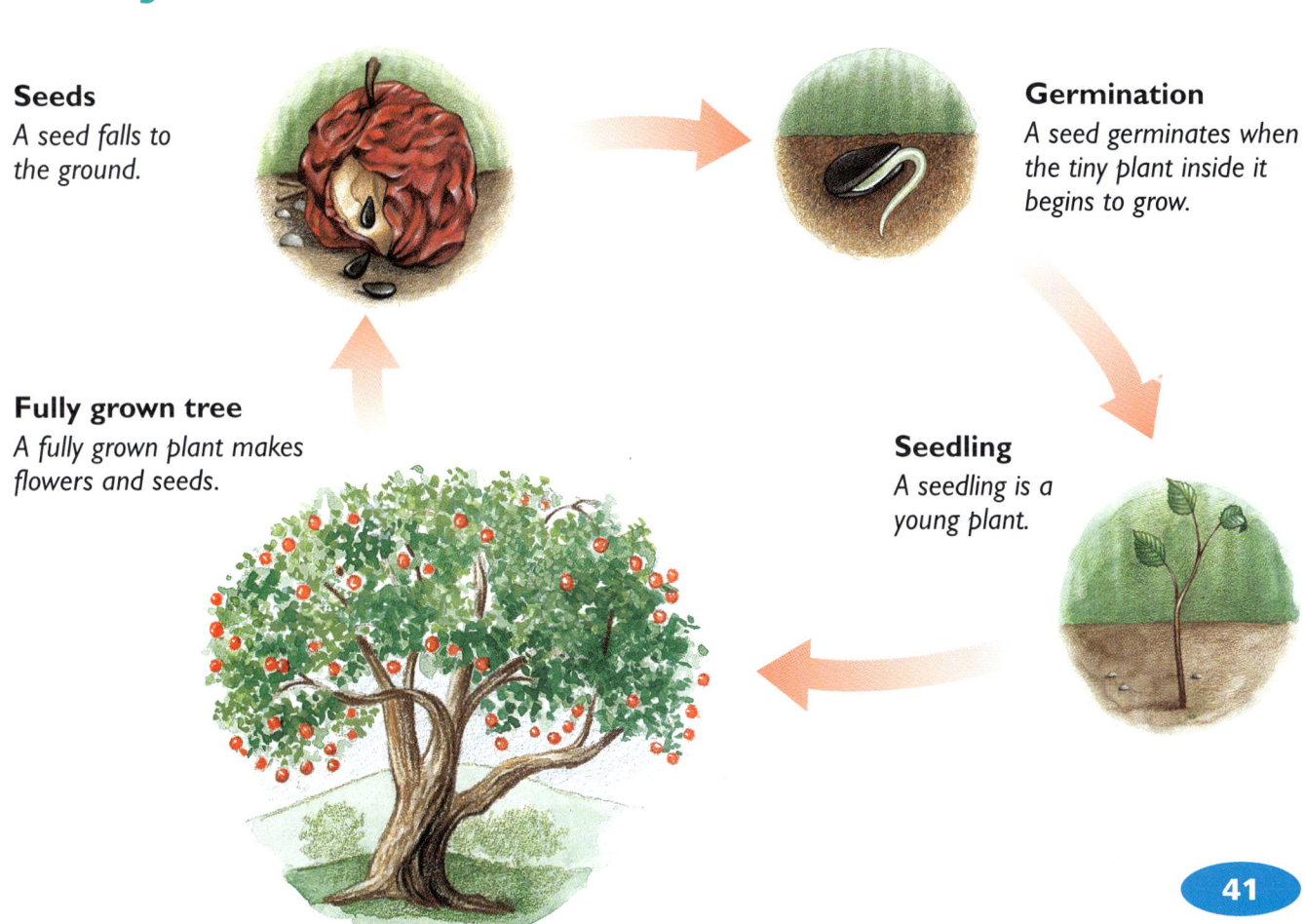

Seeds
A seed falls to the ground.

Germination
A seed germinates when the tiny plant inside it begins to grow.

Seedling
A seedling is a young plant.

Fully grown tree
A fully grown plant makes flowers and seeds.

Cells, Tissues, Organs, and Body Systems

The human body is made of small units that join together to form larger and more complicated units.

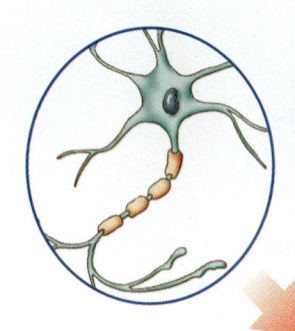

◀ A cell is the basic unit of an organism. The body has many different kinds of cells. Each kind of cell does a different job. This cell is a nerve cell.

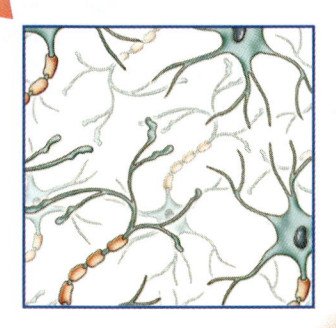

◀ A group of the same kind of cells forms a tissue. A group of bone cells forms bone tissue, and a group of muscle cells forms muscle tissue. This diagram shows how nerve cells form nervous tissue.

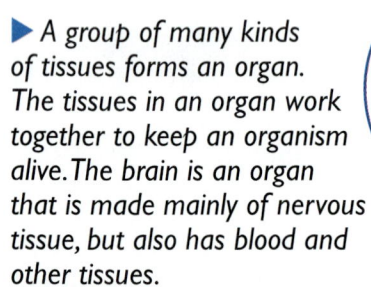

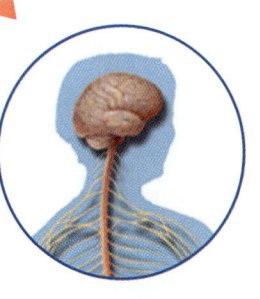

▶ A group of many kinds of tissues forms an organ. The tissues in an organ work together to keep an organism alive. The brain is an organ that is made mainly of nervous tissue, but also has blood and other tissues.

▶ Different organs work together to do a job in the body. The organs that work together to do a special job make up a system. The brain, spinal cord, and nerves make up the nervous system.

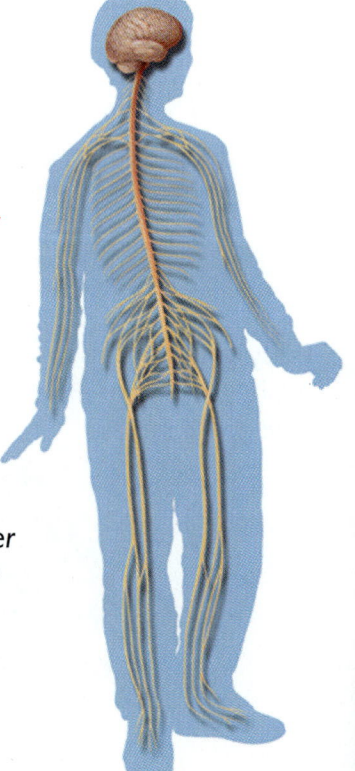

Body Systems

Each system in the human body has a special job to do.

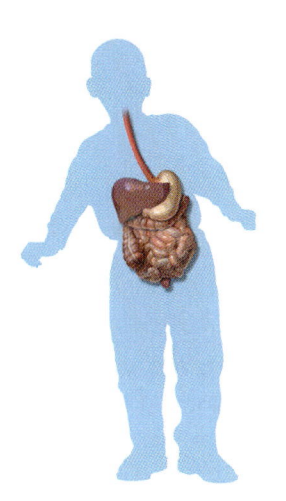

▲**Digestive System**
This system changes food into a form that body cells can use.

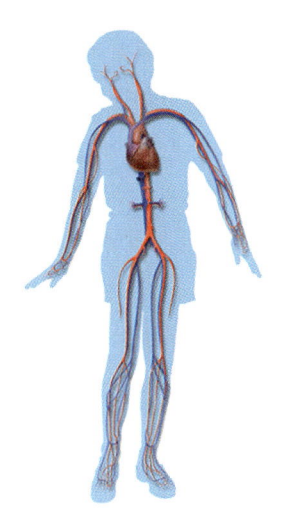

▲**Circulatory System**
This system brings oxygen and nutrients to cells and takes away wastes.

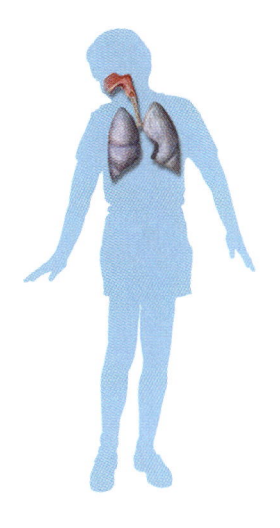

▲**Respiratory System**
This system brings oxygen into the body and gives off waste gases.

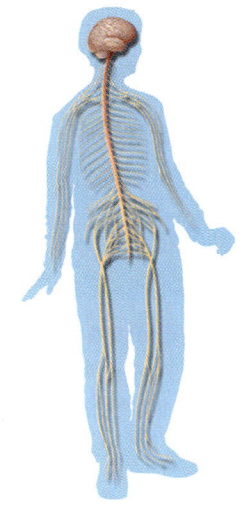

▲**Nervous System**
The brain and nerves control everything the body does.

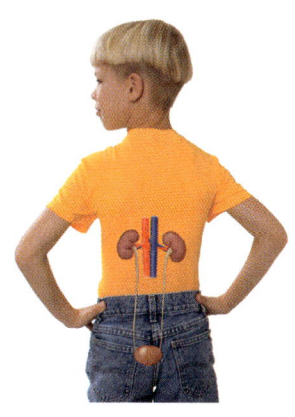

▲**Excretory System**
This system carries waste products out of the body.

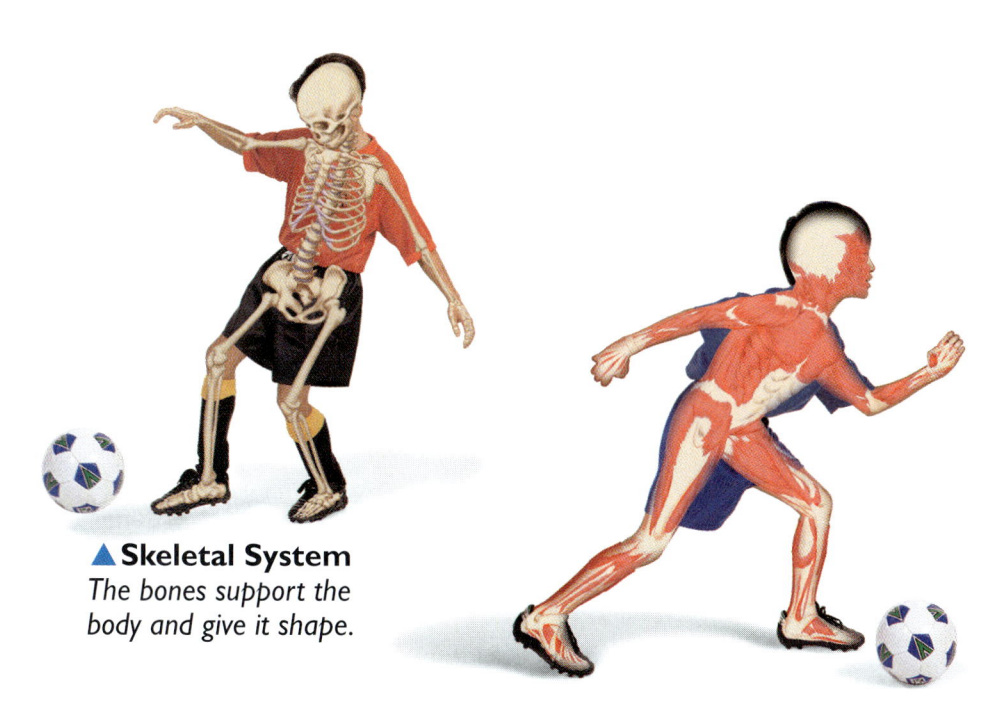

▲**Skeletal System**
The bones support the body and give it shape.

▲**Muscular System**
Muscles make body parts move and give the body shape.

43

Plant and Animal Cells

A cell is the smallest part that makes up a living thing. Plant and animal cells are different in some ways and alike in others. An animal cell contains a cell membrane, a nucleus, and cytoplasm. A plant cell contains a cell membrane, a nucleus, cytoplasm, a cell wall, and chloroplasts.

Animal Cell

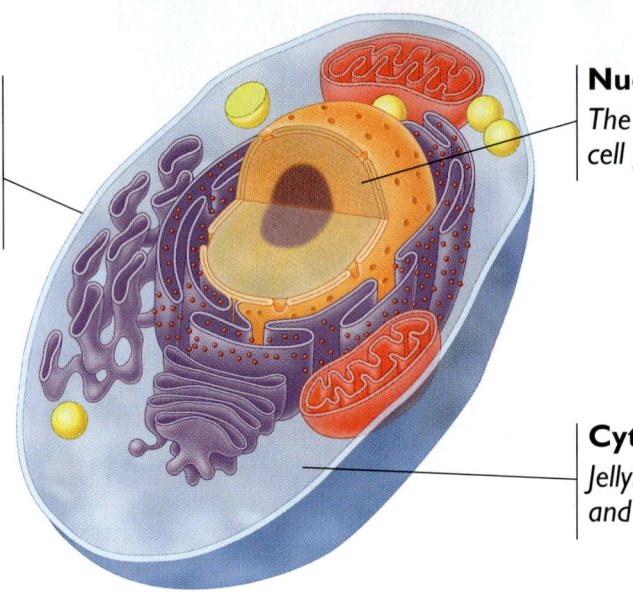

Cell Membrane
The cell membrane controls what goes in and out of the cell.

Nucleus
The nucleus directs the way the cell grows, develops, and divides.

Cytoplasm
Jellylike cytoplasm fills the cell and surrounds the nucleus.

Plant Cell

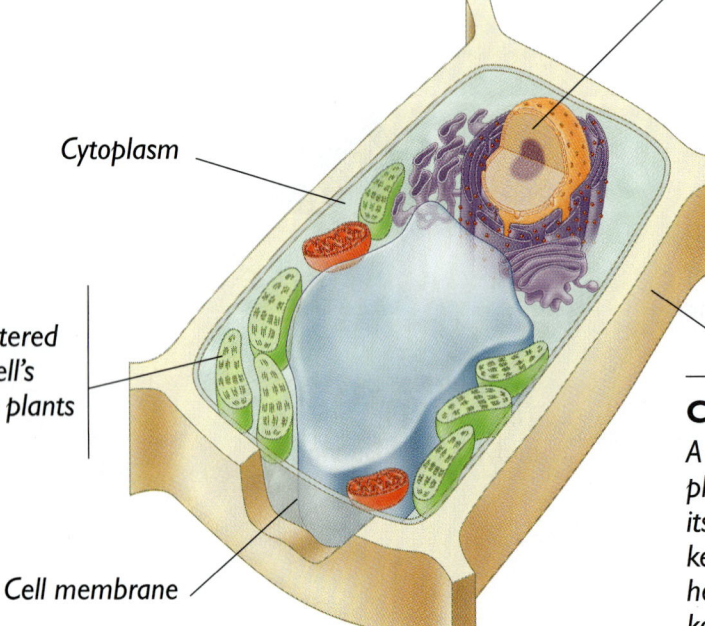

Nucleus

Cytoplasm

Chloroplast
Chloroplasts are scattered throughout a plant cell's cytoplasm. They give plants their green color.

Cell Wall
A stiff wall surrounds a plant cell just outside its cell membrane. It keeps the cell rigid and helps the whole plant keep its shape.

Cell membrane

Tools

Tools can make objects appear larger. They can help you measure volume, temperature, length, distance, and mass. Tools can help you figure out amounts and analyze your data. Tools can also provide you with the latest scientific information.

You can figure amounts using a calculator.

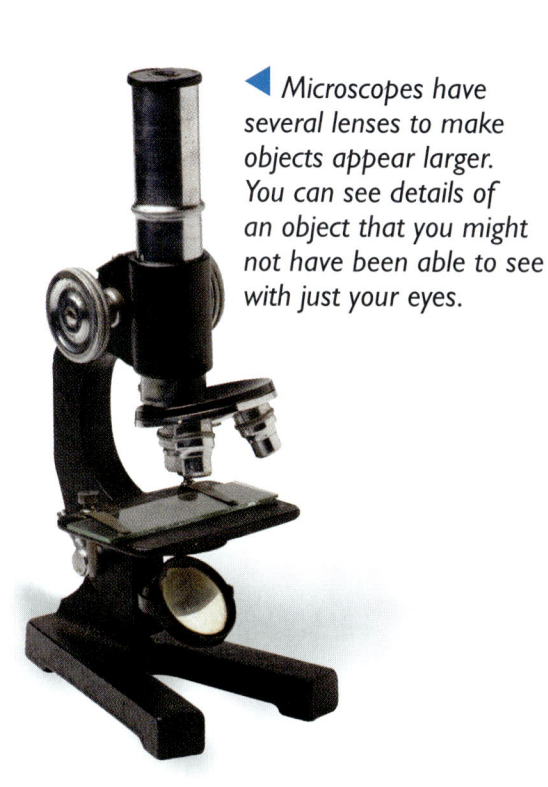

▲ *Safety goggles protect your eyes.*

◄ *Microscopes have several lenses to make objects appear larger. You can see details of an object that you might not have been able to see with just your eyes.*

▲ *A hand lens makes objects appear larger so you can see more details.*

45

▲ Computers can quickly provide the latest scientific information.

▶ You use a thermometer to measure temperature. Many thermometers have both Farenheit and Celsius scales. Usually scientists only use the Celsius scale when measuring temperature.

Scientists use metric rulers and meter sticks to measure length and distance. Scientists use the metric units of meters, centimeters, and millimeters to measure length and distance. ▼

Pictures taken with a camera record what something looks like. You can compare pictures of the same object to show how the object might have changed. ▼

46

Clocks and stopwatches are used for measuring time. ▶

You can talk into a tape recorder to record information you want to remember. You can also use a tape recorder to record different sounds. ▲

▲ *You use a balance to measure mass.*

▲ *You can use a magnet to test whether an object is made of certain metals such as iron.*

▲ *A compass is used to indicate direction. The directions on a compass include north, south, east, and west.*

47

History of Science

8000 B.C.   **6000 B.C.**   **4000 B.C**   **2000 B.C.**

Life Science

Physical Science

3000 B.C. The Egyptians develop geometry. They use it to re-measure their farmlands after floods of the Nile River.

Earth Science

8000 B.C. Farming communities start as people use the plow for farming.

Human Body

48

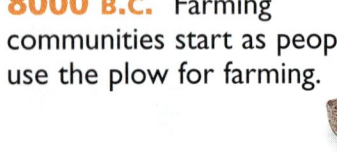

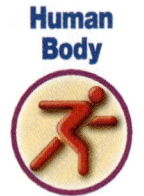

500 B.C.　　　400 B.C.　　　300 B.C.　　　200 B.C.　　　100 B.C.

4th century B.C.
Aristotle classifies plants and animals.

3rd century B.C.
Aristarchus proposes that the earth revolves around the sun.

4th century B.C.
Aristotle describes the motions of falling bodies. He believes that heavier things fall faster than lighter things.

260 B.C. Archimedes discovers the principles of buoyancy and the lever.

4th century B.C. Aristotle describes the motions of the planets.

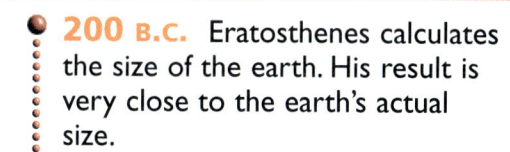

200 B.C. Eratosthenes calculates the size of the earth. His result is very close to the earth's actual size.

87 B.C.
Chinese report observing an object in the sky that later became known as Halley's comet.

5th and 4th centuries B.C.
Hippocrates and other Greek doctors record the symptoms of many diseases. They also urge people to eat a well-balanced diet.

49

110 AD   235   360   485   610   735

Life Science

Physical Science

83 A.D. Chinese travelers use the compass for navigation.

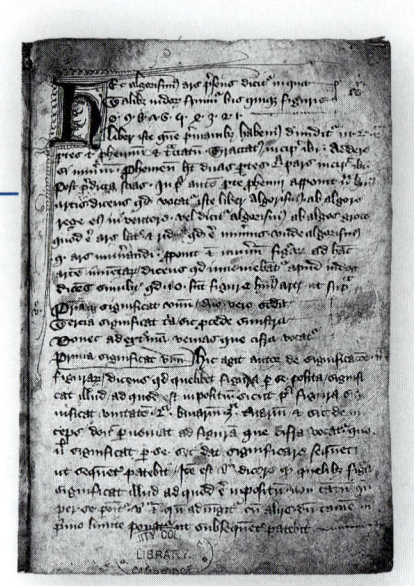

About 750–1250 Islamic scholars get scientific books from Europe. They translate them into Arabic and add more information.

Earth Science

140 Claudius Ptolemy draws a complete picture of an earth-centered universe.

132 The Chinese make the first seismograph, a device that measures the strength of earthquakes.

Human Body

2nd century Galen writes about anatomy and the causes of diseases.

860　　　**985**　　　**1110**　　　**1225**　　　**1250**　　　**1475**

1100s
Animal guide books begin to appear. They describe what animals look like and give facts about them.

1250
Albert the Great describes plants and animals in his book *On Vegetables and On Animals*.

1555
Pierre Belon finds similarities between the skeletons of humans and birds.

9th century
The Chinese invent block printing. By the 11th century, they had movable type.

1019
Abu Arrayhan Muhammad ibn Ahmad al'Biruni observed both a solar and lunar eclipse within a few months of each other.

1543
Nikolaus Copernicus publishes his book *On The Revolutions of the Celestial Orbs*. It says that the sun remains still and the earth moves in a circle around it.

1265
Nasir al-Din al-Tusi gets his own observatory. His ideas about how the planets move will influence Nikolaus Copernicus.

About 1000
Ibn Sina writes an encyclopedia of medical knowledge. For many years, doctors will use this as their main source of medical knowledge. Arab scientist Ibn Al-Haytham gives the first detailed explanation of how we see and how light forms images in our eyes.

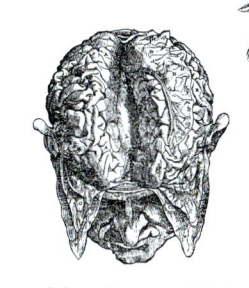

1543
Andreas Vesalius publishes *On the Makeup of the Human Body*. In this book he gives very detailed pictures of human anatomy.

51

1600 **1620** **1640** **1660** **1680**

Life Science

1663 Robert Hooke first sees the cells of living organisms through a microscope. Antoni van Leeuwenhoek discovers bacteria with the microscope in 1674.

1679 Maria Sibylla Merian paints the first detailed pictures of a caterpillar turning into a butterfly. She also develops new techniques for printing pictures.

Physical Science

1600 William Gilbert describes the behavior of magnets. He also shows that the attraction of a compass needle toward North is due to the earth's magnetic pole.

1632 Galileo Galilei shows that all objects fall at the same speed. Galileo also shows that all matter has inertia.

1687 Isaac Newton introduces his three laws of motion.

Earth Science

1609–1619 Johannes Kepler introduces the three laws of planetary motion.

1610 Galileo uses a telescope to see the rings around the planet Saturn and the moons of Jupiter.

1669 Nicolaus Steno sets forth the basic principles of how to date rock layers.

1650 Maria Cunitz publishes a new set of tables to help astronomers find the positions of the planets and stars.

1693–1698 Maria Eimmart draws 250 pictures depicting the phases of the moon. She also paints flowers and insects.

1687 Isaac Newton introduces the concept of gravity.

Human Body

1628 William Harvey shows how the heart circulates blood through the blood vessels.

52

1700   **1720**   **1740**   **1760**   **1780**   **1800**

1735 Carolus Linnaeus devises the modern system of naming living things.

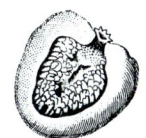

1704 Isaac Newton publishes his views on optics. He shows that white light contains many colors.

1759 Emile du Châtelet translates Isaac Newton's work into French. Her work still remains the only French translation.

1789 Antoine-Laurent Lavoisier claims that certain substances, such as oxygen, hydrogen, and nitrogen, cannot be broken down into anything simpler. He calls these substances "elements."

1729 Stephen Gray shows that electricity flows in a straight path from one place to another.

1781 Caroline and William Herschel (sister and brother) discover the planet Uranus.

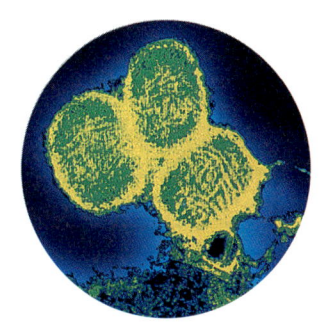

1784 French chemist Antoine-Laurent Lavoisier does the first extensive study of respiration.

1798 Edward Jenner reports the first successful vaccination for smallpox.

1721 Onesimus introduces to America the African method for inoculation against smallpox.

53

1805   1810   1815   1820   1825   1830   1835

Life Science

1808 French naturalist Georges Cuvier describes some fossilized bones as belonging to a giant, extinct marine lizard.

1838–1839 Matthias Schleiden and Theodor Schwann describe the cell as the basic unit of a living organism.

Physical Science

1800 Alessandro Volta makes the first dry cell (battery).

1820 H.C. Oersted discovers that a wire with electric current running through it will deflect a compass needle. This showed that electricity and magnetism were related.

1808 John Dalton proposes that all matter is made of atoms.

Earth Science

1830 Charles Lyell writes *Principles of Geology*. This is the first modern geology textbook.

1803 Luke Howard assigns to clouds the basic names that we still use today—cumulus, stratus, and cirrus.

Human Body

1840   1845   1850   1855   1860   1865   1870   1875

1842 Richard Owen gives the name "dinosaurs" to the extinct giant lizards.

1859 Charles Darwin proposes the theory of evolution by natural selection.

1863 Gregor Mendel shows that certain traits in peas are passed to succeeding generations in a regular fashion. He outlines the methods of heredity.

1847 Hermann Helmholtz states the law of conservation of energy. This law holds that energy cannot be created or destroyed. Energy only can be changed from one form to another.

1842 Christian Doppler explains why a car, train, plane, or any quickly moving object sounds higher pitched as it approaches and lower pitched as it moves away.

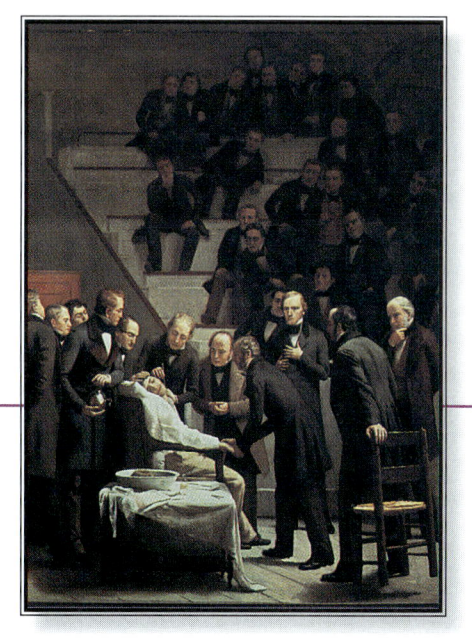

1866 Ernst Haeckel proposes the term "ecology" for the study of the environment.

Early 1860s Louis Pasteur realizes that tiny organisms cause wine and milk to turn sour. He shows that heating the liquids kills these germs. This process is called pasteurization.

1840s Doctors use anesthetic drugs to put their patients to sleep.

1850s and 1860s Ignaz P. Semmelweis and Sir Joseph Lister pioneer the use of antiseptics in medicine.

| | 1875 | 1885 | 1895 | 1905 |

Life Science

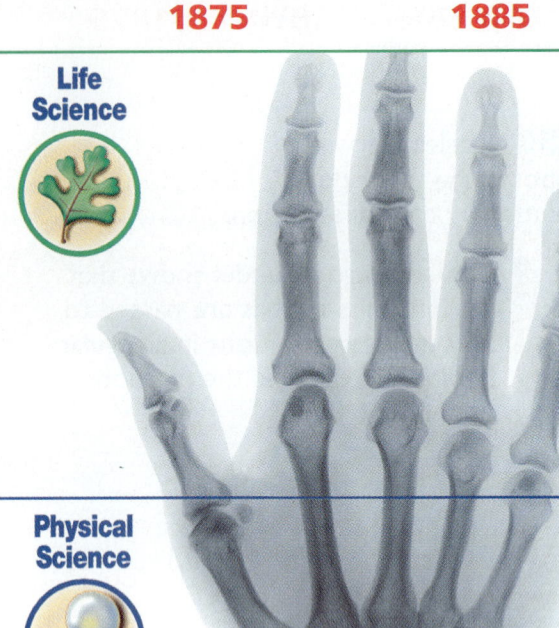

1900–1910 George Washington Carver, the son of slave parents, develops many new uses for old crops. He finds a way to make soybeans into rubber, cotton into road-paving material, and peanuts into paper.

Physical Science

1895 Wilhelm Roentgen discovers X rays.

1896 Henri Becquerel discovers radioactivity.

1897 J. J. Thomson discovers the electron.

1905 Albert Einstein introduces the theory of relativity.

Earth Science

1907 Bertram Boltwood introduces the idea of "radioactive" dating. This allows geologists to accurately measure the age of a fossil.

1912 Alfred Wegener proposes the theory of continental drift. This theory says that all land on the earth was once a single mass. It eventually broke apart and the continents slowly drifted away from each other.

Human Body

1885 Louis Pasteur gives the first vaccination for rabies. Pasteur thought that tiny organisms caused most diseases.

56

1915   **1925**   **1935**   **1945**

- **1920s** Ernest Everett Just performs important research into how cells metabolize food.

- **1947** Archaeologist Mary Leakey unearths the skull of a *Proconsul africanus*, an example of a fossilized ape.

- **1913** Danish physicist Niels Bohr presents the modern theory of the atom.
- **1911** Ernst Rutherford discovers that atoms have a nucleus, or center.
- **1911** Marie Curie wins the Nobel Prize for chemistry. This makes her the first person ever to win two Nobel Prizes, the highest award a scientist can receive.

- **1938** Otto Hahn and Fritz Straussman split the uranium atom. This marks the beginning of the nuclear age.
- **1942** Enrico Fermi and Leo Szilard produce the first nuclear chain reaction.
- **1945** The first atomic bomb is exploded in the desert at Alamogordo, New Mexico.
- **1938** Lise Meitner and Otto Frisch explain how an atom can split in two.

- **1933** Meteorologist Tor Bergeron explains how raindrops form in clouds.

- **1946** Vincent Schaefer and Irving Langmuir use dry ice to produce the first artificial rain.

- **1917** Florence Sabin becomes the first woman professor at an American medical college.
- **1928** Alexander Fleming notices that the molds in his petri dish produced a substance, later called an antibiotic, that killed bacteria. He calls this substance penicillin.
- **1935** Chemist Percy Julian develops physostigmine, a drug used to fight the eye disease glaucoma.
- **1922** Doctors inject the first diabetes patient with insulin.

57

1950 **1955** **1960** **1965** **1970**

Life Science

1951 Barbara McClintock discovers that genes can move to different places on a chromosome.

1953 The collective work of James D. Watson, Francis Crick, Maurice Wilkins, and Rosalind Franklin leads to the discovery of the structure of the DNA molecule.

1972 Researchers find human DNA to be 99% similar to that of chimpanzees.

Physical Science

1969 UCLA is host to the first computer node of ARPANET, the forerunner of the internet.

1974 Opening of TRIUMF, the world's largest particle accelerator, at the University of British Columbia.

Earth Science

1957 The first human-made object goes into orbit when the Soviet Union launches *Sputnik I*.

1969 Neil Armstrong is the first person to walk on the moon.

1967 Geophysicists introduce the theory of plate tectonics.

1962 John Glenn is the first American to orbit the earth.

1972 Cygnus X-1 is first identified as a blackhole.

Human Body

1954–1962 In 1954, Jonas Salk introduced the first vaccine for polio. In 1962, most doctors and hospitals substituted Albert Sabin's orally administered vaccine.

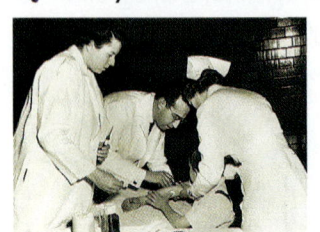

1967 Dr. Christiaan Barnard performs the first successful human heart transplant operation.

1964 The surgeon general's report on the hazards of smoking is released.

NO SMOKING

58

1975   **1980**   **1985**   **1990**   **1995**   **2000**

1988
Congress approves funding for the Human Genome Project. This project will map and sequence the human genetic code.

1997
Scientists in Edinburgh, Scotland, successfully clone a sheep, Dolly.

1975 People are able to buy the first personal computer, called the Altair.

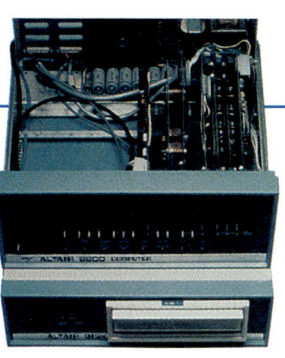

1996 Scientists make "element 112" in the laboratory. This is the heaviest element yet created.

1979 A near meltdown occurs at the Three Mile Island nuclear power plant in Pennsylvania. This alerts the nation to the dangers of nuclear power.

1995 The first "extra-solar" planet is discovered.

Early 1990s The National Severe Storms Laboratory develops NEXRAD, the national network of Doppler weather radar stations for early severe storm warnings.

1976 National Academy of Sciences reports on the dangers of chlorofluorocarbons (CFCs) for the earth's ozone layer.

1981 The first commercial Magnetic Resonance Imaging scanners are available. Doctors use MRI scanners to look at the non-bony parts of the body.

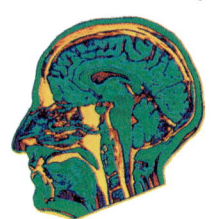

1982 Dr. Stanley Prusiner identifies a new kind of disease-causing agent—prions. Prions are responsible for many brain disorders.

1998 John Glenn, age 77, orbits the earth aboard the space shuttle *Discovery*. Glenn is the oldest person to fly in space.

59

Glossary

Full Pronunciation Key

The pronunciation of each word is shown just after the word, in this way: **ab•bre•vi•ate** (ə brē′vē āt).

The letters and signs used are pronounced as in the words below.

The mark ′ is placed after a syllable with primary or heavy accent, as in the example above.

The mark ′ after a syllable shows a secondary or lighter accent, as in **ab•bre•vi•a•tion** (ə brē′vē ā′shən).

a	hat, cap	g	go, bag	ō	open, go	ŦH	then,	zh	measure,
ā	age, face	h	he, how	ȯ	all, caught		smooth		seizure
â	care, fair	i	it, pin	ô	order	u	cup, butter		
ä	father, far	ī	ice, five	oi	oil, voice	u̇	full, put	ə	represents:
b	bad, rob	j	jam, enjoy	ou	house, out	ü	rule, move		a in about
ch	child, much	k	kind, seek	p	paper, cup	v	very, save		e in taken
d	did, red	l	land, coal	r	run, try	w	will,		i in pencil
e	let, best	m	me, am	s	say, yes		woman		o in lemon
ē	equal, be	n	no, in	sh	she, rush	y	young, yet		u in circus
ėr	term, learn	ng	long, bring	t	tell, it	z	zero,		
f	fat, if	o	hot, rock	th	thin, both		breeze		

A

absorb (ab sôrb′), to take in.

adaptation (ad′ap tā′shən), any structure or behavior that helps a living thing meet its need for survival.

air mass (âr mas), a large body of air that has about the same temperature and humidity throughout.

air pressure (âr presh′ər), the amount that air presses or pushes on anything.

amphibian (am fib′ē ən), one of a large group of animals with backbones that live part of their lives in water and part on land.

amplify (am′plə fī), to make stronger.

anemia (ə nē′mē ə), a condition in which the number of healthy red blood cells or the amount of hemoglobin is low.

anemometer (an′ə mom′ə tər), a tool that measures wind speed.

artery (ar′tər ē), the kind of blood vessel that carries blood away from the heart.

asteroid (as′tə roid′), a rocky object orbiting the sun between the planets.

atherosclerosis (ath′ər ō sklə rō′sis), a disease in which fatty substances build up on the inside walls of arteries.

atrium (ā′trē əm), one of two spaces in the top part of the heart that receive blood from veins.

axis (ak′sis), an imaginary line through a spinning object.

B

backbone, the main bone, made up of many small bones joined together, that runs along the middle of the back in some animals.

balance (bal′əns), an instrument used to measure an object's mass.

bar graph (graf), a graph that uses bars to show data.

barometer (bə rom′ə tər), a tool that measures air pressure.

behavior (bi hā′vyər), the way a living thing acts.

boiling (boi′ling) **point**, the temperature at which matter changes from a liquid to a gas.

bullhorn (bùl′hôrn′), an instrument with a built-in microphone that makes sound louder.

C

camouflage (kam′ə fläzh), any coloring, shape, or pattern that allows a living thing to blend into its surroundings.

capacity (kə pas′ə tē), the amount a container can hold.

capillary (kap′ə ler′ē), a tiny blood vessel with thin walls through which oxygen, nutrients, and wastes pass.

carbon dioxide (kär′bən dī ok′sīd), a gas found in air.

carnivore (kär′nə vôr), a consumer that eats other consumers.

cause (kòz), a person, thing, or event that makes something happen.

centimeter (sen′tə mē′tər), a metric unit used to measure length; 1/100 of a meter.

chemical (kem′ə kəl) **change**, a change in matter that produces a different kind of matter.

chemical (kem′ə kəl) **energy**, energy that comes from chemical changes.

chlorophyll (klôr′ə fil), the green substance found in plants that traps energy from the sun and gives plants their green color.

classify (klas′ə fī), to sort into groups based on similarities and differences.

colony (kol′ə nē), a kind of animal group in which each member has a different job.

comet (kom′it), a frozen chunk of ice and dust that orbits the sun.

compass (kum′pəs), a small magnet that can turn freely.

complex machine (kom′pleks mə shēn′), a machine made of many simple and compound machines.

compound machine (kom′pound mə shēn′), a machine made of two or more simple machines.

concave lens (kon kāv′ lenz), a lens that is thinner in the middle than at the edges.

concussion (kən kush′ən), a condition caused by a sudden movement of the brain inside the skull, usually involving a brief loss of consciousness.

condense (kən dens′), to change from a gas to a liquid state.

conductor (kən duk′tər), a material through which electric current passes easily.

conifer (kon′ə fər), a plant that makes seeds inside cones.

constellation (kon′stə lā′shən), a group of stars that form a pattern.

consumer (kən sü′mər), a living thing that gets energy by eating plants and other animals.

context (kon′tekst), the parts directly before or after a word or sentence that influence its meaning.

continental (kon′tə nen′tl) **shelf**, the shallow part of the ocean at the edge of the continents.

continental (kon′tə nen′tl) **slope**, the edge of the continental shelf that extends steeply downward to the ocean floor.

control, the part of an experiment that does not have the variable being tested.

convex lens (kon veks′ lenz), a lens that is thicker in the middle than at the edges.

coral reef (kôr′əl rēf), a platform or ridge of coral at or near the ocean surface.

cubic meter (kyü′bik mē′tər), a unit for measuring the volume of a solid.

current (kėr′ənt), a riverlike flow of water in the ocean.

D

dark zone, the ocean water where sunlight does not reach.

decomposer (dē′kəm pō′zər), a consumer that puts materials from dead plants and animals back into the soil, air, and water.

density (den′sə tē), how much mass is in a certain volume of matter.

dicot (dī′kot) **seed**, a seed that has two seed leaves that contain stored food.

digestion (də jes′chən), the changing of food into forms that the body can use.

dormant (dôr′mənt), the resting stage of a seed.

dune (dün), a pile of sand formed by the wind.

E

earthquake (ėrth′kwāk′), the shaking of the ground caused by rock movement along a fault.

ecosystem (ē′kō sis′təm), all the living and nonliving things in an environment and how they interact.

effect (ə fekt′), whatever is produced by a cause; a result.

electric signal (i lek′trik sig′nəl), a form of energy.

electrical (i lek′trə kəl) **energy**, energy that comes from the flow of electricity.

electromagnet (i lek′trō mag′nit), a magnet made when an electric current flows through a wire.

ellipse (i lips′), the shape of a flattened circle.

embryo (em′brē ō), a tiny part of a seed that can grow into a new plant.

endangered (en dān′jərd), having a population that is falling low in number and that is in danger of becoming extinct.

energy (en′ər jē), the ability to do work.

enzyme (en′zīm), a chemical that helps your digestive system change food into nutrients.

erosion (i rō′shən), the moving of weathered rocks and soil by wind, water, or ice.

esophagus (i sof′ə gəs), the tube that carries food and liquids from the mouth to the stomach.

exoskeleton (ek′sō skel′ə tən), a hard outer covering that supports and protects some animals without backbones.

extinct (ek stingkt′), no longer existing.

F

fault (fȯlt), a crack in the earth's crust along which rocks move.

fertilization (fėr′tl ə zā′shən), the combination of sperm from a pollen grain with an egg to form a seed.

food chain, the flow of energy through a community.

food web, all the food chains in a community.

force (fôrs), a push or a pull on an object that can cause it to change motion.

forecast (fôr′kast′), a prediction of what the weather will be like.

fossil (fos′əl), any mark or remains of a plant or animal that lived a long time ago.

freezing (frē′zing) **point,** the temperature at which matter changes from a liquid to a solid.

friction (frik′shən), a force that slows the motion of moving objects.

front (frunt), the line where two air masses meet.

G

generator (jen′ə rā′tər), a machine that uses an energy source and a magnet to make electricity.

gills, organs for breathing found in fish and amphibians.

graduated cylinder (graj′ü ā′tid sil′ən dər), a tool used to measure the volume of liquids.

gram, the basic unit for measuring mass.

graphic source (graf′ik sôrs), a drawing, photograph, table, chart, or diagram that shows information visually.

gravity (grav′ə tē), a force that pulls any two objects toward one another, such as you toward the center of the earth.

H

habitat (hab′ə tat), a place where an animal or a plant lives.

hearing aid, an instrument used to help people with a hearing problem hear better.

herbivore (hėr′bə vôr), a consumer that eats plants.

hibernation (hī′bər nā′shən), a long, deep sleep in which an animal's heart rate and breathing are much slower than normal.

high blood pressure (presh′ər), a disease in which blood is pumped through the arteries with too much force.

high-pressure area (hī′ presh′ər âr′ē ə), a place where cool air sinks and pushes down on the earth's surface with more pressure.

host (hōst), a plant or animal that is harmed by a parasite.

humidity (hyü mid′ə tē), the amount of water vapor in the air.

hygrometer (hī grom′ə tər), a tool that measures humidity.

I

indigestion (in′də jes′chən), one or more symptoms, such as stomachache, that occur when the body has difficulty digesting food.

inertia (in ėr′shə), the tendency of a moving object to stay in motion or a resting object to stay at rest.

instinct (in′stingkt), a behavior that an animal is born with and does not need to learn.

insulator (in′sə lā′tər), a material through which electric current does not pass easily.

K

kilogram (kil′ə gram), a metric unit of mass equal to 1,000 grams.

kinetic (ki net′ik) **energy**, energy of motion.

L

landform, a shape of the land, such as a mountain, plain, or plateau.

large intestine (in tes′tən), the last organ of the digestive system, which removes water and stores the waste material.

light zone, the sunlit waters of the ocean.

line graph (graf), a graph that connects point to show how data change over time.

liter (lē′tər), a unit for measuring volume.

low-pressure area (lō′presh′ər âr′ē ə), a place where warm air rises and pushes down on the earth's surface with less pressure.

M

magnet (mag′nit), anything that pulls iron, steel, and certain other metals to it.

magnetic (mag net′ik) **field**, the space around a magnet where magnetism acts.

magnetism (mag′nə tiz′əm), the force around a magnet.

mammal (mam′əl), an animal with a backbone that usually has hair on its body and feeds milk to its young.

mass (mas), the amount of material that an object has in it.

matter (mat′ər), anything that has mass and takes up space.

mechanical (mə kan′ə kəl) **energy**, the kind of energy an object has because it can move or because it is moving.

median (mē′dē ən), the middle number when the data are put in order.

65

melting (mel´ting) **point,** the temperature at which matter changes from a solid to a liquid.

meteor (mē´tē ər), a piece of rock or dust from space burning up in Earth's air.

meteorite (mē´tē ə rīt´), a rock from space that has passed through Earth's air and landed on the ground.

meteorologist (mē tē ə rol´ə jist), a person who studies weather.

meter (mē´tər), a unit for measuring length.

microphone (mī´krə fōn), an instrument used to amplify voices, music, and other sounds.

migration (mī grā´shən), the movement of an animal from one location to another as the seasons change.

milliliter (mil´ə lē´tər), a unit for measuring volume equal to 1/1000 of a liter.

mineral (min´ər əl), nonliving, solid matter from the earth.

mixture (miks´chər), two or more substances that are mixed together but can be easily separated.

mode (mōd), the number that occurs most often in the data.

molt (mōlt), to shed an animal's outer covering.

monocot (mon´ə kot) **seed,** a seed that has one seed leaf and stored food outside the seed leaf.

N

National Weather Service (nash´ə nəl weᴛʜ´ər sér´vis), a government agency that collects information about weather.

nerve cell (nėrv sel), a cell that gathers and carries information in the body.

nerve ending (nėrv en´ding), a tiny branch of a nerve cell that gathers information.

nutrient (nü´trē ənt), a substance in food that the body uses for energy, for growth and repair, or for working well.

O

ocean basin (bā´sn), the floor of the deep ocean.

omnivore (om´nə vôr´), a consumer that eats both plants and other consumers.

opaque (ō pāk´), does not allow light to pass through.

orbit (ôr´bit), the path of an object around another object.

ovary (ō´vər ē), the bottom part of the pistil in which seeds form.

ovule (ō´vyül), the inner part of an ovary that contains an egg.

P

parallel circuit (par´ə lel sėr´kit), a circuit that connects several objects in a way that the current for each object has its own path.

parasite (par´ə sīt), a plant or animal that feeds off another living thing and harms it.

photosynthesis (fō´tō sin´thə sis), a process by which plants change light energy from the sun and use it to make sugar.

physical (fiz´ə kəl) **change**, a change in matter that changes physical properties, but does not produce a different kind of matter.

pistil (pis´tl), part of a flower that makes the eggs that grow into seeds.

pitch (pich), the highness or lowness of a sound.

plasma (plaz´mə), the liquid part of blood that carries nutrients, wastes, and blood cells.

platelet (plāt´lit), a small part of a blood cell that helps blood clot and stops bleeding.

pole (pōl), a place on a magnet where magnetism is strongest.

pollen (pol´ən), tiny grains that make seeds when combined with a flower's egg.

pollination (pol´ə nā´shən), the movement of pollen from a stamen to a pistil.

pollution (pə lü´shən), anything harmful added to the air, land, or water.

potential (pə ten´shəl) **energy**, energy that an object has because of position.

precipitation (pri sip´ə tā´shən), moisture that falls from clouds to the ground.

predator (pred´ə tər), an animal that hunts and kills other animals for food.

predict (pri dikt´), to tell what will happen next based on what has already happened.

prey (prā), the animals that predators hunt.

producer (prə dü´sər), a living thing that uses sunlight to make sugar.

R

rain gauge (gāj), a tool that measures precipitation.

range (rānj), the difference between the highest and lowest number in the data.

recycle (rē sī´kəl), to use the same materials over and over again.

red blood cell, the kind of blood cell that carries oxygen to other body cells.

reflect (ri flekt´), to bounce back.

reflex (rē′fleks), a simple, automatic behavior.

reproduce (rē′prə düs′), to make more of the same kind.

reptile (rep′tīl), an animal with a backbone that has a dry, scaly skin.

resistance (ri zis′təns), a measure of how much a material opposes the flow of electric current and changes electric current into heat energy.

response (ri spons′), a behavior caused by a stimulus.

revolution (rev′ə lü′shən), the movement of an object around another object.

ridge (rij), the highest part of a chain of underwater mountains.

rotation (rō tā′shən), one full spin of an object around an axis.

S

saliva (sə lī′və), the liquid in the mouth that makes chewed food wet and begins digestion.

satellite (sat′l īt), an object that revolves around another object.

scavenger (skav′ən jər), an animal that eats dead animals.

sense organ (sens ôr′gən), a body part that has special nerve cells that gather information about the surroundings.

sepal (sē′pəl), one of the leaflike parts that protects a flower bud and that is usually green.

series circuit (sir′ēz sėr′kit), a circuit that connects several objects one after another so that the current flows in a single path.

simple machine (sim′pəl mə shēn′), a machine made of one or two parts.

small intestine (in tes′tən), the organ of the digestive system in which most digestion takes place.

solar system (sō′lər sis′təm), the sun, the nine planets and their moons, and other objects that orbit the sun.

solution (sə lü′shən), a mixture in which one substance spreads evenly throughout another substance.

spinal cord (spī′nl kôrd), a thick bundle of nerves that connects the brain and nerves throughout the body.

spore (spôr), a tiny cell that can grow into a new plant.

stamen (stā′mən), part of a flower that makes pollen.

stethoscope (steth′ə skōp), an instrument used to hear the sounds of body organs.

stimulus (stim′yə ləs), the cause of a behavior.

symbiosis (sim′bē ō′sis), a special way in which two different kinds of living things live together.

T

tide, the rise and fall of the surface level of the ocean.

translucent (tran slü′snt), allows light to pass through but scatters it so that whatever is behind it cannot be clearly seen.

transmit (tran smit′), to allow to pass through.

transparent (tran spâr′ənt), allows light to pass through so that whatever is behind can be seen.

trench, a deep, narrow valley in the ocean floor.

V

vein (vān), the kind of blood vessel that carries blood back to the heart.

ventricle (ven′trə kəl), one of two spaces in the bottom part of the heart that pump blood out of the heart.

vibrate (vī′brāt), to move quickly back and forth.

visible spectrum (viz′ə bəl spek′trəm), light energy that can be seen and can be broken into the colors of the rainbow.

volcano (vol kā′nō), a mountain formed by hardened lava with an opening through which lava, ashes, rocks, and other materials come out.

volume (vol′yəm), the amount of space that matter takes up; the loudness or softness of a sound.

W

wave, the up-and-down movement of ocean water caused by the wind.

wavelength (wāv′lengkth′), the distance from a point on a wave to the same point on the next wave.

weathering (weTH′ər ing), the breaking and changing of rocks.

wind vane (vān), a tool that shows wind direction.

work (wėrk), the result of a force moving an object.

Index

A

Absorb, B99
Activities
　Explore, A6, A36, A66, A96, B6, B34, B62, B92, C6, C36, C64, C96, D6, D34,
　Investigations, A24, A44, A60, A72, A90, A112, B20, B40, B46, B72, B78, B104, B114, C24, C54, C76, C106, D18, D46, D56
　Experiments, A29, B55, B85, C89, D27
Adaptations, A98-A104, A105-A106, A108-A111, C84, C86
Advertisement (promotional material), B128, D126
　evaluating, A14-A15
Air, C12-C16
Air mass, C26
　high and low pressure, C13
　fronts, C26-C27
Air pressure, C12-C14
　measuring, C14
　weather and, C26
Amphibian, A47, 39
Amplify, B118, B119
Anemia, D40
Anemometer, C16
Animals, A38-A59, A100-A106, A108-A111, A117, A118-A119
　adaptations of, A100-A104, A105-A106, A108-A111
　with backbones, A46-A52
　without backbones, A40-A43
　behaviors of, A56-A57
　cell of, 44
　care of young, A48, A50, A52, A53, A106, A107
　characteristics from parents, A54-A57
　classification of, A38-A52
　extinct, A118-A119
　groups of, A105-A106
　habitats of, A70-A71, C84-C87
　life cycles of, A27-A29, A49, A53, 8
　saltwater habitats of, C84-C87
　in soil, C53
Annelid, 38
Arachnid, 38
Arctic Ocean, C66
Artery, D14
Asteroid, C118
Atherosclerosis, D42
Atlantic Ocean, C66, C79
Atmosphere, C116, 2
Atrium, D16
Axis (of earth), C98

B

Backbone, A39
Balance, 47
Ballard, Robert, C71
Bar graphs, making, A37
Barometer, C14
Battery (dry cell), B66, B67
Behavior, A56, A57, A58
Bending (of light), B102-B103
Birds, A50-A51, 39
Blood, D13-D14
Boiling point, B23
Brain, B118, D20, 10
　effect of drugs on, D53, D54
Bullhorn, B118, B119

C

Calculator, 45
Camera, using, A126, C72, C78, D63
Camouflage, A102-A104
Capacity, exploring, D7
Capillary, D15
Carbon dioxide, A75
　in air, A75
　and plants, A8, A75
Careers, A28, A70, A71, A72, B118, B119, C28, C47, C72

astronaut, C70, C102
doctor, B118
engineer, C75
farmer, A28, C47
firefighter, B119
meteorologist, C28
nurse, B118
oceanographer, C70, C71, C72, C78
photographer, C72
Carnivore, A78, A79
Cause and effect, identifying, B63, D35
Cell membrane, 44
Cell wall, 44
Cells (human body), 42
Centimeter, B13
Charts, making and using, A125, C126
Chemical change, B26-B29
Chemical energy, B29, B44
Chlorophyll, A74
Chloroplast, 44
Circulatory system, D13-D17
   and drugs, D45
   problems of, D40-D42
   and tobacco, D44
Cirrus clouds, C19
Classifying, A9, A14, 10-11
Clay, C52-C53
Climate, 3
   zones of, 3
Clouds, C17-C19
   types of, C18-C19
Cnidarian, 38

Cold front, C27
Collecting data, xv
Colony, A106
Comets, C119
Communicating, 8-9
Compass, B76, 47
Complex machine, B54
Compound machine, B52-B53
Computer, 46
Concave lens, B103
Concussion, D49
Condensation, C22
Conductor, B67
Conifer, A11
Conservation, C58-C59
Constellation, C120-C121
Consumer, A77
Context clues, using, A67
Continental shelf, C68
Continental slope, C68
Control, 26-27
Convex lens, B103
Cooling, B24
   and changing matter, B24-B25
Coral reef, C87
Core (of earth), 2
Cousteau, Jacques, C70
Craters, C118
Crust (of earth), 2
Crustacean, 38
Cubic meter, B14
Cumulus clouds, C19

Current (ocean), C78-C80
Cytoplasm, 44

D

Dark zone (ocean), C85, C86
Data, collecting and interpreting, 24-25
Decomposers, A81
Deep Flight project, C74
Density, B18-B19
Dicot seed, A22
Digestion, D8
Digestive system, D8-D12
   problems of, D36-D37
Dormant, A26
Dune, C46

E

Ear, B116-B117, B121
Eardrum, B117
Earle, Sylvia, C71, C75
Earth, C38-C59, C98-C101, C108-C113
   eclipses, C104
   gravity and, C99
   layers of, 2
   light and shadows on, C9, C100, C101, C104
   and moon, C102-C103
   movement of, C98-C99
   nature of, C108
   resources from, C56-C57
   and solar system, C108-C117
   sun and, C98-C101

Earthquakes, C42–C43
    California and, C42–C43
    protection against, C43
    San Andreas fault, C42
    tracking of, C43
Eclipses, C104–C105
Ecosystem, A68–A71
Electric charge, B64–B65
Electric circuits, B67, B68–B69
    parallel, B69
    series, B68–B69
Electric current, B66–B67, B68–B69
Electric signal, B118, B119
Electrical energy, B45
Electricity, B64–B71, B80–B84
    magnetism and, B80–B84
    safety and, B70–B71
Electromagnet, B82–B84
    uses of, B84
Ellipse, C110
El Niño, C80
Embryo, A22
Endangered, A118
    causes of, A118–A119
Energy, A8, A74–A76, A77–A81, B42–B45
    changing forms, B43, B44
    chemical, B45
    electrical, B45
    kinetic, B43
    mechanical, B44
    potential, B42

of sun, A8, A74–A76, A77
and work, B48–B49
Environment, A114–A117
    and pollution, A114–A115
    protection of, A116–A117
    and recycling, A117
Enzyme, D9
Erosion, C46–C47, C112
Esophagus, D10, D11
Estimating, 12–13
Evaluate research and technology, A127
Evaporation, C22
Evidence of the past, 6
    similarities to present, 6
Excretory system, 11
Exoskeleton, A42
Experimenting, 28–29
Extinct, A118
    animals and plants, A118–A119
Eye, D24

F

Fault, C42
Fern, A12–A13
Fertilization, A20–A21
Fish, A46–A47
    around coral reefs, C87
    in ocean dark zone, C86
    in ocean light zone, C86
Flash floods, C31
    safety during, C31
Flowers, A15–A21

Food, A23, D8, D9, D36, D37
    digestion of, D8
    healthful, D39
    from plants and animals, A23
Food chain, A82–A83
    changes in, A86–A88
Food poisoning, D37
Food web, A84–A88
Force, B36–B39
Forecast, C28
Forecasting weather, C28–C29
Formulating questions and hypotheses, 22–23
Fossils, A120–A121
    of extinct organisms, 6
    similarities to present-day, 6
Freezing point, B24
Friction, B38–B39
Front, C26–C27
    cold, C27
    warm, C27
Fruit, A23

G

Gases, B9, B23, C40
    solids versus, B9, B23
    in volcanoes, C40
Generator, B81
Germinate, A26, A27
Gilbert, William, B76
Gills, A47
Glacier, C46

Graduated cylinder, B15
Gram, B17
Graphic sources, using, A127, B93, B127, C125, D61, D62
Graphs, making and using, A127, B127, D62
Gravity, B37, C99
   Earth and, C99
   solar system and, C110
Gulf Stream, C79

H

Habitats, A70-A71, C84-C87
   loss of, A88, A89
Hand lens, 45
Hawkes, Graham, C75
Hearing aids, B120-B121
Heart, D16-D17
Heat, B23
   changing state and, B23
Herbivore, A78, A79
Hibernation, A109
High blood pressure, D41
   prevention of, D44
High-pressure area, C13
History of science, B12, B38, B76, B82, B120, C66, C72-C73, 48-59
Hive (of insects), A105
H.M.S. *Challenger*, C72
Host, A110
Human body, D8-D26, D36-D55
   cells, tissues, organs of, 10
   systems of, D8-D12, D13-D17, D20-D26
   keeping systems healthy, D38-D39, D43-D45, D48-D50, D54-D55
Humidity, C21
   air masses and, C26
   measuring, C21
Hurricanes, C30, C31
   safety during, C31
   warnings, C31
Hygrometer, C21
Hypothesis, xv

I

Igneous rock, C50, 10
Illegal drugs, D54
Inclined plane, B50
Indian Ocean, C66
Indigestion, D36-D37
   prevention of, D38-D39
Inertia, B38, B39
Inferring, 14-15
Insects, A42, 8
Instinct, A56, A57
Insulator, B67
Invention, D126
Invertebrates, 38

J

JASON project, C74
Jupiter, C109, C110-C111, C114-C115
   Galileo mission to, C114-C115
   moons of, C115

K

Kilogram, B17
Kilometer, B13
Kinetic energy, B43

L

Landforms, C38-C39
   erosion and, C46
   rocks and, C39
   volcanoes, earthquakes and, C40-C43
   weathering and, C44-C45
Large intestine, D10, D11
Laser light, B97
Lava, C40, C41
Learned behavior, A58-A59
Length, B12-B13
Lens, B103, D24
Lever, B51
Life cycles, A27-A29, A49, A53, 40–41
   of butterfly, 41
   of frog, 40
   of garter snake, A49
   of gerbil, A53
   of sea turtle, A49
   of tree, 41
Light, B94-B103
   and bending, B102-B103
   and color, B95, B98

and different materials, B98
and eyes, D24, B99
and heat, C8-C10
and lenses, B103
and mirrors, B100-B101
nature of, B94, B96, B98
sources of, B94, B95
visible spectrum, B94

Light waves, B96-B97

Light zone (of ocean), C85, C86

Lightning, C30, C31, C115

Liter, B14

Lobster, A43

Lodestone, B76

Low-pressure area, C13

Lunar eclipse, C104, C105

M

Machines, B50-B54
complex machines, B54
compound machines, B52-B53
simple machines, B50-B51
as tools, B50-B51

Magma, C40

Magnet, B74
Chinese and, B76
compass and, B76
the earth as, B76-B77
Greeks and, B76

Magnetic field, B74

Magnetism, B74-B84
electricity and, B80-B84

Main idea, identifying, A7

Mammals, A52-A53
life cycles of, A53

Mantle (of earth), 2

Maps, making and using, A127, C126

Mars, C109, C110-C111, C113
spacecraft to, C113

Marsupial, 39

Mass, B8, B16-B17
exploring, B7

Matter, B8-B11
finding density, B18-B19
measuring length, B12-B13
measuring mass, B16-B17
measuring volume, B14-B15
physical properties of, B9-B10
states of, B9, B23-B24, C11

Measuring, B12-B18, B23-B24, C11

Mechanical energy, B44

Melting point, B23

Mercury, C109, C110-C111, C112
spacecraft to, C112

Meteor, C118

Meteorite, C118

Meter, B13

Meter stick, B12, B13, 46,

Metric ruler, 46

Metric system, B13, B17

Microphone, B118, B119

Microscope, 46

Mid-Atlantic Ridge, C73

Migration, A108

Milligram, B17

Milliliter, B14

Millimeter, B13

Minerals, C48-C49
colors of, C49
hardness of, C49, 5
luster of, C48
Mohs' scale of, 5
in rocks, C48
uses of C48-C49

Mixture, B10-B11

Models, making and using, A126, B81, C127, 20-21

Molt, A42

Monocot seed, A22

Moon, C102-C103, C104, C105
and eclipse, C104, C105
and gravity, C81
phases of, C102-C103
and solar system, C108
and tides, C81

Moons (of other planets), C109, C115, C116

Mosses, A12-A13

Motion, B36-B43, B48-B49

Muscular system, 11

N

National Weather Service, C29

Natural gas, C56

74

conservation, C58
renewable, C56
Natural resources, C56-C57
   conservation of, C58-C59
Neptune, C109, C110-C111, C117
   spacecraft to, C117
Nerve cell, D20-D21, 10
Nerve ending, D21, D22
Nervous system, D20
   cells, tissues, organs, of, 10
   effect of drugs on, D53, D54-D55
   preventing injuries to, D48-50
Newton, Isaac, B38
Nonrenewable resources, C56
Nose, D25
NR-1 (nuclear submarine), C73
Nucleus, 44
Nutrient, D8

O

Observing, 6-7
Ocean, C66-C88
   and air temperature, C10
   and climate, 3
   and erosion, C83
   exploration of, C70-C75
   floor of, C66, C68-C69
   as habitats, C84-C87
   movements of, C81, C82-C83,
   pollution of, A115, C88
   protection of, A117, C88
   and sounding, C67
   water pressure in, C74
Ocean basin, C68
Ocean exploration, C70-C75
   explorers of, C70-C71
   history of, C66
   projects of, C74-C75
   vessels of, C72-C73
Oersted, Hans, B82
Omnivore, A78, A79
Opaque, B99
Operational definitions, making, 18-19
Orbit, C99, C119
   of comets, C119
   of Earth, C99
   of moon, C102
   of Pluto, C111
Organs (of nervous system), 10
Ovary (in plants), A20, A21, A23
Over-the-counter medicine, D53
Ovule (in plants), A20, A21

P

Pacific Ocean, C66, C80
Parallel circuit, B69
Parasite, A110
Petroleum, C57
   conservation of, C58
   as renewable resource, C57
Photosynthesis, A75
Physical change, B22-B25
Physical properties, B9-B10
Piccard, Auguste, C70
Piccard, Jacques, C70
Pistil, A16, A17, A18, A19, A20, A21
Pitch (of sound), B110
Planets, C108-C117
Plants, A8-A28, A98-A99, A118-A119
   adaptations of, A98-A99
   cell of, 44
   classification of, A8-A14
   energy of, A8, A74-A76
   extinct, A118-A119
   life cycle of, A27-A29, 8
   parts of, A16-A17, A26
   seeds of, A10, A22, A23, A26, A27
Plasma, D13
Platelets, D13
Pluto, C109, C110-C111, C117
Poles (in magnet), B75
Pollen, A16, A17, A18
Pollination, A19-A21
Pollution, A87, A115
Potential energy, B42
Precipitation, C20-C21
Predator, A83
Predicting, C28-C29, C97, 16-17

75

Prescription medicine, D53
    safe use of, D53
Pressure (of air), C12-C14
Pressure (of ocean), C74
Prey, A83
Pride (of lions), A106
Problem solving, A97, C65
    using logical reasoning, C65
Producer, A76
Pulley, B51

R

Radar image maps, C28
Rain, C20
    air masses and, C26
    and cold fronts, C27
    and erosion, C47
    formation of, C20
Rain gauge, C21
Range, mode,
    and median, C7
Ray (of light), B100-B102
Recycle, A117
Recycling (of water), C22-C23
Red blood cells, D13
Reflect, B99
Reflex, A57
Renewable resource, C56
Reproduce, A9, A12
Reptile, A48, 39
Resistance, C56-C57

Resources, C56-C57
    conservation of, C58-C59
    nonrenewable, C56
    renewable, C56, C57
Respiratory system, 11
Response, A57
Revolution (of Earth), C99
Ridge (of ocean), C69
Rocks, C50-C51
    cycle of, C50-C51, 34
    formation of, C50-C51
    kinds of, C50-C51
    as resources, C50-C51
Rotation (of Earth), C98

S

Safety goggles, 45
Safety in science, B70-B71, C30-C31, 2-3
Saliva, D9
Sand, C52-C53
Satellites, C102
    natural satellites, C102
    photos and, C78
    and ocean mapping, C67, C78
    and weather forecasts, C29
Saturn, C109, C110-C111, C116
    Voyager missions to, C116
Scavenger, A80
School (of fish), A105
Science inquiry, xvi

Science process skills, xiv
    observing, xiv
    classifying, xiv
    inferring, xiv
    communicating, xiv
    estimating and measuring, xiv
    predicting, xv
    making and using models, xv
    collecting and interpreting data, xv
    making operational definitions, xv
    formulating questions and hypotheses, xv
    identifying and controlling variables, xv
Science tools, 45-47
    balance, 47
    calculator, 45
    camera, A126, C72, C78, C63, 46
    clock or stopwatch, 47
    compass, B76, B12, B13, 47
    computer, 46
    hand lens, 45
    magnet, B74, 47
    meter stick or metric ruler, 46
    microscope, B10, 45
    safety goggles, 45
    tape recorder, A126, C127, 46
    thermometer, B23, C11, C72, 46
Scientific methods,
    state the problem, xii

formulate your hypothesis, xii
identify and control variables, xii
test your hypothesis, xiii
collect your data, xiii
interpret your data, xiii
state your conclusion, xiii
inquire further, xiii
for experimenting, A29, B55, B85, C89, C27

Screw, B51
Seasons, C100, C101
Sedimentary rock, C51, 10
Sediments, C51
Seeds, A10, A22, A23, A26, A27
Sense organs, D20
Sepal, A16, A17
Series circuit, B68-B69
Shadows, C9, C104-C105
    movement of, C9
Simple machines, B50-B51
Skeletal system, 43
Skin, D22
Small intestine, D10, D11
Snow, C18, C20
    formation of, C20
    winter storm safety, C31
Soil, C52-C53
    and ability to hold water, C52-C53
    importance of, C52-C53
    formation of, C52
    kinds of, C52-C53
    and plant growth, C52-C53
    properties of, C52-C53
Solar eclipse, C104
Solar system, C108, C109-C111, C118-C120
    and other objects, C118-C120
    and planets, C108-C111
Solution, B11
Sound, B106-B121
    and different materials, B112-B113
    and hearing, B116-B117, B120-B121
    how made, B106-B107
    and noise pollution, B111
    properties of, B108-B111, B118-B119
Space missions, C114-C115, C116-C117
Space probes, C112-C113
Spinal cord, D22
Spore, A12
Stamen, A16, A17, A18
Stars, C120-C121
    constellations, C120-C121
    sun as a, C120
Stethoscope, B118
Stimulus, A57
Stopwatch, 47
Stratus clouds, C18
Submarines, C73

Sun, A74, A75, B95, C8-C10, C17, C85, C99, C100, C102-C103, C104, C120
    and Earth, C8-C10, C99, C101,
    eclipse of, C104
    energy from, A74, A75, C8, C85, C120
    and evaporation, C17, C22
    light from, A75, B95, C85, C99
    and moon, B95, C102-C103, C104
    and solar system, C110-C111
Sunlight, A75, A100, C8, C99, C101, C104, C120
    direct vs. indirect, C8, C100
    and heating earth, C8-C10, C100, C101, C120
Supporting facts and details, identifying, C37
Survival, A98-A111
    and adaptations, A98-A111, A114-A117
Systems, C50-C51, C22-C23, C68-C71, C110-C111, D8-D12, D13-D17, D20-D26, 10
    of human body, D8-D12, D13-D17, D20-D26
    living and nonliving, A68-A71

77

of planets, C110–C111
  rock cycle, C50–C51, 10
  in space, C98–C99, C110–C111
  water cycle, C22–C23
Symbiosis, A110–A111

T

Tape recorder, A126, C127, 46
Taste bud, D25
Technology, using, B120–B121, C28–C29, C43, C70, C72, C73, C74, C75, C78, C112–C117, C120, D17
  evaluating use of, A127, C127
Telescope, C117, C120
  Hubbell, C117
Temperature, B23–B24, C11
  climate and, 3
  and different surfaces, C10
  measuring, B23, C11
Thermometer, B23, C11, C72, 46
Thunderstorms, C30, C31
  safety during, C31
  warnings of, C30
Tide (of ocean), C81
Tongue, D25
Topsoil, C52–C53
Tornadoes, C30
  safety during, C30
  warnings of, C30
Translucent, B98

Transmit, B99
Transparent, B98
Trees (as resource), C57
  conservation of, C59
  renewable resource, C57
Trench (of ocean), C69

U

Uranus, C109, C110–C111, C116
  Voyager mission to, C116

V

Variables, identifying and controlling, 26–27
Vein, D15
Ventricle, D16
Vertebrate, 39
Vibrate, B106–B107
Visible spectrum, B94
Venus, C109, C110–C111, C112
Volcanoes, C40–C41, C112
Volume, B8
  measurement of, B14–B15
  and sound, B109

W

Walsh, Don, C70
Warm front, C27
Water cycle, C22–C23
Water erosion, C83
Water vapor, C17
  and clouds, C17
  and humidity, C21

Wave (of ocean), C82–C83
Wavelength, B96, B108
Weather, C8–C31
  predicting, C28–C29
  and radar maps, C28
  and safety, C30–C31
Weather maps, C28
Weathering, C44–C45
Wedge, B50
Weight, exploring, B35
Wheel and axle, B50
White blood cells, D13
Wind, C13, C15–C16
  and air pressure, C13
  and high and low pressure, C13
Wind direction, C15
Wind speed, C15, C115
Wind vane, C15
Winter, C100–C101
Winter storm, C31
  safety during, C31
  warning, C31
Word problems, solving, A97, C65
Work, B48–B49
Writing for Science, A128, B128, C128, D64
  researching a topic, A128
  outlining and writing a report, B128
  using drawings to show information, C128

Acknowledgments

Illustration
Borders Patti Green; **Icons** Precison Graphics

Front Matter J.B. Woolsey

Unit A 20, 27d, 74, 78, 108 Precision Graphics; 22, 27a-d J.B. Woolsey; 39c Ka Botzis; 70a Walter Stuart

Unit B 50 Walter Stuart; 78, 100, 101, 108, 109a, 112, 113, 117, 121 J.B. Woolsey

Unit C 9, 12, 13, 14, 27, 99, 100, 103b, 104 J.B. Woolsey; 40a, 53, 66, 67, 68, 79, 81 Precision Graphics

Unit D 11, 15, 23 Precision Graphics; 16, 21, 22, 24, 26 J.B. Woolsey; 42 Christine D. Young

Photography
Unless otherwise credited, all photographs are the property of Scott Foresman, a division of Pearson Education. Page abbreviations are as follows: (T) top, (C) center, (B) bottom, (L) left, (R) right, (INS) inset.

Cover: Lynette Cook/SPL/Photo Researchers; **iv** PhotoDisc, Inc.; **v** T Joe McDonald/DRK Photo; **v** B Michael Fogden/Animals Animals/Earth Scenes; **viii-ix** Background Leo L. Larson/Panoramic Images

Unit A
1 Spencer Jones/Bruce Coleman Inc.; **2** T Vincent O'Bryne/Panoramic Images; **2** CL Arie deZanger for Scott Foresman; **2** CR Arie deZanger for Scott Foresman; **2** Inset Nick Caloyianis; **3** C John Pade/Nelson/Pade Multimedia; **3** B Michael Stuwe; **8** David Young-Wolff/PhotoEdit; **9** William M. Smithey, Jr./Planet Earth Pictures (Seaphot Ltd.); **9** Inset John Neubauer/PhotoEdit; **10** B PhotoDisc, Inc.; **12** T Bill Beatty/Animals Animals/Earth Scenes; **13** T Runk/Schoenberger/Grant Heilman Photography; **13** T-Inset Runk/Schoenberger/Grant Heilman Photography; **14** TR Breck P. Kent/Animals Animals/Earth Scenes; **14** B Jim Corwin/Photo Researchers; **18** William J. Weber/Visuals Unlimited; **20** B Runk/Schoenberger/Grant Heilman Photography; **21** BL Mary Goljenboom/Ferret Research, Inc.; **21** BC Mary Goljenboom/Ferret Research, Inc.; **21** BR Mary Goljenboom/Ferret Research, Inc.; **38** Tom Bean/Tony Stone Images; **39** T Superstock, Inc.; **39** B R. Maler/IFA/Bruce Coleman Inc.; **40** T Zig Leszczynski/Animals Animals/Earth Scenes; **40** B Bob and Clara Calhoun/Bruce Coleman Inc.; **41** T Chris McLaughlin/Animals Animals/Earth Scenes; **41** C E. S. Ross; **41** B Chris McLaughlin/Animals Animals/Earth Scenes; **42** Bill Beatty/Visuals Unlimited; **42** Inset L. West/Photo Researchers; **43** T Jane Burton/Bruce Coleman Inc.; **43** C Frans Lanting/Minden Pictures; **43** B Tom McHugh, 1973, Steinhart Aquarium/Photo Researchers; **45** BR John Gerlach/Dembinsky Photo Assoc. Inc.; **45** TL James P. Rowan/DRK Photo; **45** CL Scott Camazine/Photo Researchers; **45** CR E. R. Degginger/Bruce Coleman Inc.; **45** BL Kramer/Stock Boston; **45** TR D. Lyons/Bruce Coleman Inc.; **46** PhotoDisc; **47** T Gary Meszaros/Dembinsky Photo Assoc. Inc.; **47** B Mark Moffett/Minden Pictures; **48** T Joe McDonald/DRK Photo; **48** B Wayne Lankinen/DRK Photo; **49** TR Mitsuaki Iwago/Minden Pictures; **49** CR Wolfgang Bayer/Bruce Coleman Inc.; **49** CL Frans Lanting/Minden Pictures; **49** BR Marty Cordano/DRK Photo; **50** T PhotoDisc, Inc.; **50** B Art Wolfe/Tony Stone Images; **51** T Stephen Dalton/Animals Animals/Earth Scenes; **51** BL Dr. E. R. Degginger/Color-Pic, Inc.; **51** BR D. Cavagnaro/Visuals Unlimited; **52** Chuck Davis/Tony Stone Images; **53** T Renee Stockdale/Animals Animals/Earth Scenes; **53** C Julian Barker/National Gerbil Society; **53** B Julian Barker/National Gerbil Society; **54** Robert Maier/Animals Animals/Earth Scenes; **55** Leen Van Der Slik/Animals Animals/Earth Scenes; **56** T Steve Maslowski/Photo Researchers; **56** B Michio Hoshino/Minden Pictures; **57** T Leroy Simon/Visuals Unlimited; **58** Ralph Reinhold/Animals Animals/Earth Scenes; **59** Pat & Tom Leeson/DRK Photo; **63** Art Wolfe/Tony Stone Images; **68** L-Inset C. C. Lockwood/Animals Animals/Earth Scenes; **68** B PhotoDisc, Inc.; **68** R-Inset John Gerlach/DRK Photo; **75** Jose Carillo/PhotoEdit; **77** Lee Rentz/Bruce Coleman Inc.; **78** B Patti Murray/Animals Animals/Earth Scenes; **78** T Kim Taylor/Bruce Coleman Inc.; **79** T M.H. Sharp/Photo Researchers; **79** BR PhotoDisc, Inc.; **79** BL Zig Leszczynski/Animals Animals/Earth Scenes; **79** CR Norman Owen Tomalin/Bruce Coleman Inc.; **80** CL Tim Laman/Wildlife Collection; **80** TL Joe McDonald/Visuals Unlimited; **82** R Rod Planck/TOM STACK & ASSOCIATES; **82** L Michael Gadomsky/Photo Researchers; **83** BL-inset Larry West/Photo Researchers; **83** R-Inset David Northcott/Superstock, Inc.; **83** Background Peter Cade/Tony Stone Images; **84** T Rod Planck/TOM STACK & ASSOCIATES; **84** CL Michael Gadomsky/Photo Researchers; **84** CR John Cancalosi/TOM STACK & ASSOCIATES; **84** B Tom Vezo/Wildlife Collection; **85** TL © Heather Angel ; **85** TC Larry West/Photo Researchers; **85** CL Lynn M. Stone; **85** TCR David Northcott/Superstock, Inc.; **85** CC Stephen J. Krasemann/DRK Photo; **85** CR Michael Durham/ENP Images; **85** BL Dwight R. Kuhn/DRK Photo; **85** BR Stephen J. Krasemann/DRK Photo; **86** C Tony Freeman/PhotoEdit; **86** BL Michael Gadomsky/Photo Researchers; **86** BR Rod Planck/TOM STACK & ASSOCIATES; **87** L Larry West/Photo Researchers; **87** R David Northcott/Superstock, Inc.; **88** T David W. Harp Photographer; **88** BR Norman Tomalin/Bruce Coleman Inc.; **88** CL Frans Lanting/Minden Pictures; **89** T Patti Murray/Animals Animals/Earth Scenes; **89** CL Steve Winter/National Geographic; **89** CR Steve Winter/National Geographic; **93** Lee Rentz/Bruce Coleman Inc.; **98** R Peter Feibert/Liaison Agency; **98** L Bill Gallery/Stock Boston; **99** T Clifton Carr/Minden Pictures; **99** B Ken Cole/Animals Animals/Earth Scenes; **100** T HPH Photography/Wildlife Collection; **100** B Bruce Coleman Inc.; **101** T © Heather Angel ; **101** C John W. Matthews/DRK Photo; **101** B Michael Fogden/Animals Animals/Earth Scenes; **102** T Jim Brandenburg/Minden Pictures; **102** B Dr. Paul A. Zahl/Photo Researchers; **103** TR Frans Lanting/Minden Pictures; **103** CL Frans Lanting/Minden Pictures; **103** BR Jim Brandenburg/Minden Pictures; **104** B Fred Bavendam/Minden Pictures; **104** T Patti Murray/Animals Animals/Earth Scenes; **105** Scott Camazine/Photo Researchers; **106** B HPH Photography/Wildlife Collection; **106** T Erwin and Peggy Bauer/Bruce Coleman Inc.; **107** B ZEFA-Bauer/Stock Market; **107** T Mitsuaki Iwago/Minden Pictures; **108** L Francois Gohier/Photo Researchers; **108** C Patti Murray/Animals Animals/Earth Scenes; **108** R Dave B. Fleetham Marine Photographer/Visuals Unlimited; **109** T Jeff Foott/Bruce Coleman Inc.; **109** B Wayne Lankinen/Bruce Coleman Inc.; **110** TL Bradley Simmons/Bruce Coleman Inc.; **110** TR E.R. Degginer/Animals Animals/Earth Scenes; **110** BL F. Stuart Westmorland/Photo Researchers; **110** BR M.C. Chamberlain/DRK Photo; **111** T Art Wolfe Inc.; **111** B Zig Leszczynski/Animals Animals/Earth Scenes; **114** Owen Franken/Stock Boston; **115** T Townsend P. Dickinson/Image Works; **115** B Warren Williams/Planet Earth Pictures (Seaphot Ltd.); **116** Background Johnathan Nourok/PhotoEdit; **116** TR Michael Newman/PhotoEdit; **116** B Tony Freeman/PhotoEdit; **116** TL Richard Hutchings/Photo Researchers; **117** T Bob Daemmrich/Stock Boston; **117** B Greg Vaughn/TOM STACK & ASSOCIATES; **118** Mark J. Thomas/Dembinsky Photo Assoc. Inc.; **119** B John Obata/The National Tropical Botanical Garden, Lawai, Kauai, Hawaii; **119** C J. Beckett/American Museum of Natural History/Department of Library Services, Neg. No. 5367(4); **119** T Tom McHugh/Photo Researchers; **121** T Field Museum of Natural History, Chicago, IL/Neg.#GE086127C, photograph by John Weinstein; **121** B David M. Dennis/TOM STACK & ASSOCIATES; **123** HPH Photography/Wildlife Collection; **125** PhotoDisc, Inc.

Unit B
1 Tom Pantages; **2** T Vincent O'Bryne/Panoramic Images; **2** C Geoff Tompkinson/SPL/Photo Researchers; **3** B Alan L. Detrick/Photo Researchers; **3** C Dennis Potokar/Photo Researchers; **7** Kim Brownfield; **24** PhotoDisc, Inc.; **25** TL Binney & Smith; **25** TR Richard T. Nowitz/National Geographic; **25** CL Richard T. Nowitz/National Geographic; **25** CR Richard T. Nowitz/National Geographic; **29** NASA; **36** Al Bello/Tony Stone Images; **37** Milt & Joan Mann/Cameramann International, Ltd.; **38** Myrleen Ferguson/PhotoEdit; **42** Tony Freeman/PhotoEdit; **45** Jim Shippee/Unicorn Stock Photos; **48** Robert Clay/Visuals Unlimited; **77** Pekka Parviainen/SPL/Photo Researchers; **93** Michael Giannechini/Photo Researchers; **94** Michael Giannechini/Photo Researchers; **95** B Bruce Coleman Inc.; **95** C Robert E. Daemmrich/Tony Stone Images; **97** Background Lowell Georgia/Science Source/Photo Researchers; **97** TR-Inset Alfred Pasieka/Science Photo Library/Photo Researchers; **97** BR-inset Will and Deni McIntyre/Photo Researchers; **101** L Jeremy Horner/Tony Stone Images; **103** T Richard Megna/Fundamental Photographs; **103** C Richard Megna/Fundamental Photographs; **108** Mark Richards/PhotoEdit; **109** Myrleen Ferguson/PhotoEdit; **111** T Tony Stone Images; **112** T Harold Hoffman/Photo Researchers; **112** B Flip Nicklin/Minden Pictures; **118** Tom McCarthy/PhotoEdit; **119** BR Milt & Joan Mann/Cameramann International, Ltd.; **119** TR David Young-Wolff/Tony Stone Images; **120** T Hulton Deutsch Collection Ltd.; **120** B Hulton-Deutsch Collection/Corbis Media; **121** BR Jane Shemilt/Science Photo Library/Photo Researchers; **121** TL Jane Shemilt/Science Photo Library/Photo Researchers; **121** TR G. Thomas Bishop/Custom Medical Stock Photo

Unit C
1 Frank Siteman/PhotoEdit; **2** T Vincent O'Bryne/Panoramic Images; **2** CL NASA/Science Source/Photo Researchers; **3** B NASA; **3** C Hank Morgan/Rainbow; **8** PhotoDisc; **10** Greg Vaughn/Tony Stone Images; **15** T Felicia Martinez/PhotoEdit; **16** Barry L. Runk/Grant Heilman Photography; **17** Michael von Ruber/International Stock; **18** Craig Aurness/Corbis-Westlight; **19** T David R. Frazier/Photo Researchers; **19** BL John Lemker/Animals Animals/Earth Scenes; **20** T Mary Fulton/Tony Stone Images; **20** BL PhotoDisc, Inc.; **20** BR Johnny Johnson/DRK Photo; **27** Background Warren Faidley/International Stock; **28** L GOES Image/NOAA; **28** R GOES Image/NOAA; **29** Inset European Space Agency/Photo Researchers; **29** Ken Biggs/Tony Stone Images; **30** B Warren Faidley/International Stock; **30** T Charles Doswell III/Tony Stone Images; **31** Margaret Durrance/Photo Researchers; **37** Richard J. Green/Photo Researchers; **38** Leo L. Larson/Panoramic Images; **39** T Werner Forman/Corbis Media; **41** C Roger Werth/Woodfin Camp & Associates; **41** B Richard J. Green/

79

Photo Researchers; **41** T Kevin Schafer; **42** Inset David Parker/SPL/Photo Researchers; **42** M. Justice/Image Works; **43** Superstock, Inc.; **44** James P. Rowan Stock Photography; **45** PhotoDisc, Inc.; **46** © Heather Angel ; **47** Grant Heilman/Grant Heilman Photography; **48** L Bob Daemmrich/Stock Boston; **49** BC-Inset Dr. E. R. Degginger/Color-Pic, Inc.; **49** BL Martin Rogers/Tony Stone Images; **49** TCL&TCR Jeff J. Daly/Visuals Unlimited; **49** TL E. R. Degginger/Color-Pic, Inc.; **49** BR E. R. Degginger/Color-Pic, Inc.; **50** Inset E. R. Degginger/Color-Pic, Inc.; **50** PhotoDisc; **51** TR Breck P. Kent/Animals Animals/Earth Scenes; **51** TL E. R. Degginger/Color-Pic, Inc.; **51** BL IFA/Bruce Coleman Inc.; **51** BR Scala/Art Resource; **52** T Charlton Photos, Inc.; **56** Inset Ron Heflin/AP/Wide World; **56** Gay Bumgarner/Tony Stone Images; **57** B Mickey Gibson/Animals Animals/Earth Scenes; **57** C Index Stock Imagery; **57** T Superstock, Inc.; **61** Scala/Art Resource; **62** Inset "From the IMAX® film Titanica, © Imax Corporation/Undersea Imaging International Ltd. & TMP (1991) Limited Partnership"; **67** Dr. Ken MacDonald/'Science Photo Library/Photo Researchers; **70** T Bates Littelhales/National Geographic Image Collecttion ; **71** T Al Giddings/Ocean Images, Inc.; **71** B Emory Kristof/National Geographic Image Collection; **72** T DRK Photo; **72** B Claus Meyer/Black Star; **73** C-inset Robert Ballard/Institute for Exploration/National Geographic Image Collection; **73** T Rod Catanach/Woods Hole Oceanographic Institution; **73** B Woods Hole Oceanographic Institution; **73** B-Inset "From the IMAX® film Titanica, © Imax Corporation/Undersea Imaging International Ltd. & TMP (1991) Limited Partnership"; **73** C United States Navy; **73** T-Inset Robert Hessler/Planet Earth Pictures; **74** L Jason Project; **74** R Quest Group/Woods Hole Oceanographic Institution; **75** Amos Nachoum/Corbis Media; **78** January climatological mean sea surface temperature (Levitus et al, 1994). From http://ingrid.ldgo.colombia.edu/SOURCES/.LEVITUS94/MONTHLY+.temp/figviewer.htlm?map.url=X+Y+fig-+colors+and+fig; **80** T Elizabeth Dalziel/AP/Wide World; **80** B Marilyn Kazmers/Shark Song; **81** C Richard Chesher/Planet Earth Pictures (Seaphot Ltd.); **81** T Richard Chesher/Planet Earth Pictures ; **82** Robert Brown/International Stock; **83** R.W. Gerling/Visuals Unlimited; **84** Breck P. Kent/Animals Animals/Earth Scenes; **85** T Greg Vaughn/TOM STACK & ASSOCIATES; **85** B Jeff Foott/Bruce Coleman Inc.; **86** T Flip Nicklin/Minden Pictures; **86** CL Flip Nicklin/Minden Pictures; **86** CR Dave B. Fleetham/Visuals Unlimited; **86** B Norbert Wu; **87** Chris Huss/Wildlife Collection; **88** John Halas/FKNMS; **88** Inset Dick Harrison/FKNMS; **93** Greg Vaughn/TOM STACK & ASSOCIATES; **97** Digital Stock; **101** Digital Stock; **102** Digital Stock; **105** T John Dudak/Phototake; **108** NASA; **109** TL USGS/USRA/CASS Lunar & Planetary Institute; **109** TR J.T. Trauger(JPL), J.T. Clarke(Univ. of Michigan), the WFPC2 science team, and/NASA and ESA; **109** TCL NASA; **109** TCR Jet Propulsion Laboratory/NASA; **109** BCL U. S. Geological Survey, Flagstaff, Arizona; **109** BCR NASA; **109** BL NASA; **109** BR Alan Stern(Southwest Research Institute), Marc Buie (Lowell Observatory)/NASA and ESA; **112** T Mark Robinson, Northwestern University; **112** B NASA; **113** TL NASA; **113** C NASA; **113** NASA; **114** NASA/JPL; **115** BL K. Noll (STScI), J. Spencer(Lowell Observatory)/NASA; **115** BC K. Noll (STScI), J. Spencer (Lowell Observatory)/NASA; **115** BC K. Noll (STScI), J. Spencer (Lowell Observatory)/NASA; **115** BR K. Noll (STScI), J. Spencer (Lowell Observatory)/NASA; **115** T NASA; **116** T NASA/JPL; **116** B Erich Karkoschka(University of Arizona Lunar & Planetary Lab)and/NASA; **117** Inset NASA; **117** B Alan Stern(Southwest Research Institute), Marc Buie(Lowell Observatory)/NASA and ESA; **118** Breck P. Kent/Animals Animals/Earth Scenes; **119** B MSSSO, ANU/SPL/Photo Researchers; **119** Inset Hubble Space Telescope Comet Team and NASA; **119** T Wally Pacholka; **120** T NASA; **121** National Optical Astronomy Observatories; **125** NASA

Unit D
1 Steven E. Sutton/Duomo Photography Inc. ; **2** T Vincent O'Bryne/Panoramic Images; **3** C Courtesy TetraPak; **12** CNRI/Science Photo Library/Photo Researchers; **13** Dr. Dennis Kunkel/Phototake; **14** David M. Phillips/Visuals Unlimited; **15** L From "Behold Man," Lennart Nilsson/Albert Bonniers Forlag AB; **17** Alfred Pasieka/Science Photo Library/Photo Researchers; **25** T Albert Bonniers Forlag AB; **39** T Mary Kate Denny/PhotoEdit; **40** T Dr. E Walker/Science Photo Library/Photo Researchers; **40** B Dr. E. Walker/Science Photo Library/Photo Researchers; **45** David M. Phillips/Visuals Unlimited; **48** PhotoEdit; **52** B David Young-Wolff/PhotoEdit; **54** Steve Maines/Stock Boston; **55** Tony Freeman/PhotoEdit

End Matter
4 B Bob Kalmbach, University of Michigan Photo Services; **8** John Callahan/Tony Stone Images; **8** INS John Springer Collection/Bettmann Archive; **32** NASA; **34** L Maurice Nimmo/Frank Lane Picture Agency; **34** C Maurice Nimmo/Frank Lane Picture Agency; **35** TL Biophoto Associates/Photo Researchers; **35** TC Mark A. Schneider/Visuals Unlimited; **35** TCR Ken Lucas/Visuals Unlimited; **35** TR Thomas Hunn/Visuals Unlimited; **35** BCR Ken Lucas/Visuals Unlimited; **35** BR Jose Manuel Sanchis Calvete/Corbis Media; **36** C Fritz Prenzel/Animals Animals/Earth Scenes; **36** T Field Museum of Natural History, Neg. CK30T; **36** B E. R. Degginger/Animals Animals/Earth Scenes; **37** C Raymond A. Mendez/Animals Animals/Earth Scenes; **37** TL American Museum of Natural History/Department of Library Services, Neg. No.; **37** TR John Garrett/Tony Stone Images; **37** B PhotoDisc, Inc.; **38** CL E. S. Ross; **38** T William J. Pohley/Visuals Unlimited; **38** CR Jeff J. Daly/Visuals Unlimited; **38** BL Marty Snyderman/Visuals Unlimited; **38** BC James R. McCullagh/Visuals Unlimited; **38** BR Paul B. Swarmer/Visuals Unlimited; **39** TL Joe McDonald/DRK Photo; **39** TR Joe McDonald/Visuals Unlimited; **39** C Kjell B. Sandved/Visuals Unlimited; **39** BL Marty Snyderman/Visuals Unlimited; **39** BR PhotoDisc, Inc.; **40** TL Breck P. Kent/Animals Animals/Earth Scenes; **40** TR Breck P. Kent/Animals Animals/Earth Scenes; **40** BR Zig Leszczynski/Animals Animals/Earth Scenes; **40** BL Zig Leszczynski/Animals Animals/Earth Scenes; **48** T British Museum; **48** C Metropolitan Museum of Art; **49** T Alinari/Art Resource, NY; **49** B NOAO/Lowell Observatory; **50** T Trinity College Library, Cambridge; **50** B The Granger Collection, New York; **51** R National Library of Medicine; **51** BL From "The Structure of the Human Body," 1543; **52** TL National Museum of Women in the Arts, Washington, DC; **52** TR From Robert Hooke, "Micrographia," 1665; **52** C Public Domain; **53** C JPL/NASA; **53** B London School of Hygiene & Tropical Medicine/SPL/Photo Researchers; **53** TL Public Domain; **54** TL James L. Amos/Photo Researchers; **54** TR Hugh Spencer; **54** c Mehau Kulyk/SPL/Photo Researchers; **54** B David Frazier/Photo Researchers; **55** T Courtesy Mr. G. P. Darwin, by permission of the Darwin Museum, Down House; **55** C Courtesy Southern Pacific Railroad; **55** B Harvard Medical Library, Francis A. Countway Library of Medicine; **56** TL PhotoDisc, Inc.; **56** CR UPI/Corbis-Bettmann; **56** TR Public Domain; **57** B AP/Wide World; **57** T Staatliches Museum fur Naturkunde, Stuttgart; **57** C Charles D. Winters/Timeframe Photography Inc./Photo Researchers; **57** B UPI/Corbis-Bettmann; **58** T Tim Davis/Photo Researchers; **58** C NASA; **58** BL The Granger Collection, New York; **59** TR AP/Wide World; **59** TL Computer Museum, Boston; **59** CL Tim Shaffer/AP/Wide World; **59** BL Scott Camazine/Photo Researchers; **59** BR NASA